THE GABRIEL LETTERS

For
President Bob Fisher
Best wishes,
Richard Shriver
1-30-08

THE GABRIEL LETTERS

~Advice to a Young Angel~

By
Richard V. Shriver

Library of Congress Control Number:		2006906340
ISBN 10:	Hardcover	1-4257-2533-3
	Softcover	1-4257-2532-5
ISBN 13:	Hardcover	978-1-4257-2533-4
	Softcover	978-1-4257-2532-7

To order additional copies of this book, contact:
Xlibris Corporation
1-888-795-4274
www.Xlibris.com
Orders@Xlibris.com
30553

A GUIDE TO THE TOPICS
OF THE LETTERS

DEDICATION

To my father, the late Judge Thomas A. Shriver, who died in 1986 at
the age of ninety-four. He had been the Presiding Judge of the
Tennessee State Court of Appeals. In *The Gabriel Letters*, he
is both judges in "Letter V," Judge Fairvue
as I remember him when I was a child,
and Judge Carejust as I came to know him as
father and friend when I became an adult.
RVS—1989

ACKNOWLEDGMENTS

The original idea for *The Gabriel Letters* came to me from C. S. Lewis' *The Screwtape Letters* . . . what a marvelous introduction to the ways of God, couched in the advice of a senior devil! My philosophy of life—my theology—which I have attempted to express in this book, has been molded by some wonderful teachers and friends.

John Rustin, the minister at Belmont Methodist Church when I was growing up in Nashville, convinced me that the Church should be the most important power for good in our communities. He thought that the Church should make a difference, not just be a private club for its members.

Nels F. S. Ferré was my teacher in theology. It was he who introduced me to the idea that God is *agápe*—self-sacrificing, eternal love. He challenged me to apply this idea to every aspect of life.

The writings of Harry Emerson Fosdick, founding minister of New York's Riverside Church, have been a constant inspiration to me. Dr. Fosdick's insistence, that good religion must be reasonable, has become a standard concept for me.

Dr. William McKee has pushed me to the limit! As Dean at Cumberland University, he brought me to Cumberland "to make the students think." He says that they do so in my classes only "while kicking, screaming, and squirming!" He also has encouraged me to write.

Through the years, I shared many ideas with my father. This book is lovingly dedicated to him. My mother, Attie Gene Shriver, was my source and strength. My wife, Joy, is exactly what her name implies. She is a constant amazement in her abilities to maintain a career while ever being the great homemaker, mother, and hostess to countless students and friends. Our daughter, Kendal, is a steady source of delight.

Our son, Colin, has done the art work for the book cover. It is his original pencil sketch of Michelangelo's sculpture, "The Kneeling Angel," in San Dominico Church, Bologna, Italy.

Sarrina ViAnné, who as a student helped me with the original version of this book, has returned to Cumberland as a graduate student and again has helped me revise this edition for publication.

Richard Shriver
May 2006

LIST OF CHARACTERS

Our Father	God
The Son	Jesus, the Christ
Gabriel	Senior Archangel, writer of the letters of advice
Angelique	Gabriel's nephew; new guardian to "Young Minister"; the one to whom letters are written
Young Minister	Human clergyman for whom Angelique is guardian
The Enemy	Satan
Gruelgust	Devil assigned to "Young Minister"
Thumbhand	Satan's special counselor to church officials
Superintendent Slightly	"Young Minister's" immediate superior
Bishop Tack	"Young Minister's" bishop
Twistflesh	Devil assigned to Superintendent Slightly
Beautimus	Guardian angel to Superintendent Slightly
Ceritas	Guardian angel to Bishop Tack
Mrs. Stopall	Conservative member of the Riverville Church
Mrs. Blessings	"Saint" of Riverville
Orthodoxus	Young guardian angel
St. Peter	Keeper of the Pearly Gates
Benedictus	Guardian angel to church officials
Wordsmouth	Human preacher of "wrath"
Dr. Tunnel	Human preacher caught in his own theological trap
Judge Fairvue	Human Judge
Judge Carejust	Human Judge
Professor Free Spirit	Teacher, Angel Training College
Dr. Verily Verily	President, Angel Training College

INTRODUCTION

I have great admiration for C. S. Lewis. His *Screwtape Letters*, correspondence from a very important devil to a lesser one, is a masterpiece of satanic advice. In the original preface, he refused to explain how the correspondence fell into his hands. However, in a later edition, he admitted to the ease with which his mind was twisted into the diabolical attitude, and that the words came quickly. He refused to produce any more such letters after the first were published.

Professor Lewis did suggest in the second preface that, ideally, Screwtape's advice should have been balanced by archangelic advice to a guardian angel.

Possibly an element of immodesty has caused me to want to "collect" such correspondence. But my purpose is, I think, legitimate. It is an attempt to understand humanity from the divine point of view. I am quite aware that no human can have such understanding. But the process of stepping back, looking at ourselves, our churches, and our society from the outside, and at the same time, sensing the divine concern, has been most helpful to me.

It is my firm conviction that God's kingdom will come "on earth as it is in Heaven." In the meantime, our best understanding of Heaven is that it must be like the fellowship found in a true church: a community of people gathered out of love of God and concern for each other, to serve their community and their world. It must be a gathering of creatures with their Creator, dedicated to God and His creative, redemptive love. The whole concept of guardian angels is based upon the faith that no creature is beyond redemption or outside the realm of God's love.

The question might be asked,

"Do you believe in angels and archangels and devils and such?"

The answer for me is rather complex. Historically, of course, Christians have so believed. Biblically, the concept of guardian angels for the people of God is an almost constant assumption:

Because you have made the Lord your refuge,
No evil shall befall you,
No scourge come near your tent.
For He will give His angels charge of you
To guard you in all your ways.
On their hands they will bear you up,
Lest you dash your foot against a stone.

-Psalms 91:9-12 (RSV)

And according to the Gospel of Matthew, Jesus concludes his comments about children being the greatest in the kingdom of heaven by saying:

See that you do not despise one of these little ones;
for I tell you that in heaven their angels always behold
the face of my Father who is in heaven.

-Matthew 18:10 (RSV)

Art has continually depicted angels and devils, and literature has described them.

In the present age, our religious communities do not seem to know how to talk about the presence of spiritual beings such as angels or devils. I think that we should discuss them. I am convinced that there are positive forces for good and for evil in our lives. Once I was willing to compare good and evil to light and darkness or heat and cold . . . darkness and cold being the absence of light and heat. But no longer can I explain God as an impersonal deistic force. No longer can I be satisfied with the thought of evil—that consuming force which centers on self and can dominate our lives with destructiveness—as being merely the absence of good or the absence of God. Good and evil are very real and very personal, and human lives are constantly changed by them.

As for guardian angels, does not everyone have one?

*   *   *

A note about the masculine language used in the letters:

In the letters, the Archangel Gabriel refers to God as "our Father" and "He" and "Him." The author of the letters is not implying that God is masculine or like a man. God is not masculine. God is not feminine. God is much more than both, yet not plural. In both Jewish and Christian traditions, God is singular and personal. The problem is that in the English language there are no divine pronouns, and so Gabriel uses the traditional masculine language.

I

WELCOME TO GUARDIANSHIP AND MINISTRY

Dear Angelique,

Congratulations! I want to welcome you to your new post. To be the special guardian of our son, the young minister, should bring you many hours of joy and delight. It is indeed an honor to be made guardian to a minister who is a representative of God, our Father. New in his ministry, he will have many opportunities to serve: to speak the eternal good news, to bring beauty and knowledge to communities where beauty and knowledge are unknown, to give comfort to those who can see only present grief, to stand firmly against those who live for death by their selfishness and greed—those who give in to the subtle hunger of the forces of evil.

You have been honored for your faithfulness, but the honor will not be easily maintained. Indeed, even we are inclined to expect a minister for the Church to be more than human. But he is not! Your young minister is very human! As a matter of fact, he will be a special target of our enemy, Satan; and be assured, you will have competition from the best that his world below can produce.

Remember that your young minister has not yet been given "Heaven's" eyes. He cannot see what you have seen. And you cannot show him. He has not been to the Mountain where God is, as you have. And he cannot go . . . yet. His life now is a gift from our Father, and it is our Father's hope that he will find his way to the Mountain.

I am reminded of that well-known letter which came into our hands some while back, written by my old acquaintance, Screwtape, one of our enemy's shrewdest officers. Screwtape observed of our Father,

"He cannot ravish. He can only woo."

Our Father does reveal himself to humans. He surrounds them with His care and protection—but mostly so that they will not notice it. Humans very easily take for granted beauty, love, friendship, motherhood, families, air, water, food. They usually notice these things only when they are absent. A few wise humans see them as constant gifts from our Father.

On occasion our Father speaks directly to humans. We must admit that such conversation takes place only on rare occasions—not because He is distant from them, or unfriendly—but because He has given them so many ways of protecting themselves . . . even from Him.

You see, God wants humans to be free! He knows that only as they freely choose to live, is life real. Only as they freely choose goodness, is goodness genuine. Only as they freely choose Him can there be true fellowship. I have much to say about our Father's plans for human freedom. Soon I'll tell you my "Electric Train" story, but that must come later—a later letter.

In the mean time, my nephew, you do have a difficult task. News has come to me even as I write this letter, that indeed, our enemy has assigned a new counselor to your freshly ordained human (somehow, ordination always puts him on the alert!). The counselor's name is Gruelgust and he is experienced! He has been working with Thumbhand for years, now. I am sure you know that Thumbhand is our enemy's special counselor to church officials, and you know what success Thumbhand has had!

I do not want to alarm you—only to warn you again, that ministers are human. We will be in touch with you, constantly, trusting you in every way.

Love,
Uncle Gabriel

II

THE THICK OF THE BATTLE

Dear Angelique,

My dear nephew! I had no idea that you would be thrown so quickly into the thick of battle. The war for human souls, waged by our enemy, leaves us no time to waste. We must be on our guard. I am flattered that you want my advice and appreciate your kind reply to my letter. Yes, I have had many experiences which may help me advise you in your work.

It appears that your young minister is perceived in the "Confounds" as posing a serious threat to the enemy—much more serious than I had expected. He was not a particularly great scholar during seminary, and though his superiors see some promise in him, they have not been overly impressed. He is a fine young man, but we must look carefully at the qualities in him which could pose a threat to the enemy. The report is that Satan's forces already have launched an expensive (not in the monetary sense, of course, but in the devil-power sense) attack against him.

The quality of integrity always causes an increased production of fireballs in Hell! Your young man has a strong sense of integrity. Many of our ministers have qualities of intelligence, personality, personal magnetism, good looks, preaching ability, etc. These are all qualities which the enemy can easily divert to his benefit when integrity is weak. Remember that truth is always of our Father, though often painful to humans. Real loyalty to truth—or integrity—is very difficult for humans, and not often found to the degree that your minister has it. Integrity strikes fear into the heart of the enemy, and so he must attack it with all of his demonic might.

Another quality, strong in the young man, is an unusual dedication to the Church, really believing that the Church can change a community. He is right, of course, but few humans think so. As long as earth is not Heaven (it will be, one day, remember), earth must change. Humans' hearts individually must change. Communities must change—oh there I go preaching again, an arch-angelic privilege, I suppose!

Your young minister believes that the Church can change things and has the odd (from a human point of view) notion that change is what his ministry is all about. Few things create terror in the Confounds more than such a notion. Fortunately for the enemy, the notion usually lasts for only two or three years after the minister's arrival in the field.

Here we see clearly the enemy's plan: strike dead all such arrogance as quickly as possible. The method is predictable. He has been very successful with some of your young minister's colleagues. A few, he reaches even during seminary, though seminary provides its students with good protection from devils (their power decreases in square root proportion to any growth that takes place in a human). The seminary experience, for a student, is usually a painful but very fruitful experience, and though Satan himself has assailed several of the great divinity schools, he has had little success. When human souls grow, he flees. However, as we have pointed out, graduation and ordination find the enemy ready and waiting. He meets the young parson with full diabolical force. He strikes through the deadness of a disillusioned congregation. He strikes through the young parson's desire to be successful—his ambition and need for approval. He strikes through the loneliness which comes naturally as the young man is separated from his fellow students. And he strikes through the new colleagues, whom the young man seeks out as friends on a similar mission.

As I say, the enemy has already been successful with some of these colleagues. If your young minister determines to be loyal to the high ideals and great teachings which have inspired him during his call and training, he becomes an immediate threat to those ministers who have compromised their loyalty.

The enemy, who is the master of rationalization, makes full use of this opportunity to feed dozens of ideas into the minds of those colleagues. They will first attempt to draw your young man into their way of thinking, then become suspicious of him, and then ignore him. Even the strongest of humans needs the moral support of his colleagues. I am sure that you can understand that this process is one of the enemy's most successful demoralizers. I can see that he has already started his work on your human.

My nephew, there are several possibilities that you could use in your guardianship with the young minister to help him build his defenses:

First, you must encourage a personal prayer life. Prayer is always difficult for humans, but it is devastating to the enemy. He uses his strongest demons in vain attempting to interrupt a true conversation with our Father. I must write more on prayer later, for prayer is essential in the care of your human.

Also, you must always be on the vigil to find opportunities for his fellowship with the saints: those humans, like himself, who are seeking the way of our Father—the way of life. It is from these humans that he can find valuable support and friendship. Where two or three of these humans are gathered together, the miraculous is present.

Remind him constantly of his need to study. The parish ministry lends itself easily to shallow "busy-work." Your young human must stretch his mind toward new Father-truth every earth-day, or his soul will wither.

Prayer, fellowship, and study will always be three of our Father's ways of reaching your young human and constantly supporting him in his work. You must encourage him to make these practices every earth-day habits.

I have much more advice for you, but the rehearsal of the archangelic choir is calling. You are indeed a feather off the old wing, and we are proud (not always a sin, you know).

Your loving uncle,
Gabriel

III

THE ELECTRIC TRAIN

Dear Angelique,

You have reason to be angry! That human preacher, Wordsmouth, who has been causing trouble for your young minister has been creating trouble for us as well. Our Father is also angry. I suppose He should be—it is He that is insulted by such talk.

Wordsmouth is telling all that nonsense again, about how humans (and angels) were created only to serve God. The idea is not all bad . . . it is just that his emphasis is misplaced. (We all do serve our Father, because we are dedicated to goodness and all goodness comes from God.) But Wordsmouth's emphasis is all on the servitude, suggesting slavery, and that all our Father wants is submission.

Wordsmouth does not realize what such a view implies about our Father. God's purpose in Creation is a glory. Creation is His gift. The soul (a possession of both humans and angels) is the gift of our Father's being. His purpose is to share Himself. Young Saul of Tarsus (known to humans as St. Paul) caught a vision of the gift and said with true understanding, " . . . we (humans) have obtained access to this grace in which we stand, and we rejoice in our hope of sharing the glory of God." It is the human hope that our Father promises the sharing of His glory. We, of the angelic realm, experience the glory. Very few humans have, but many hope and many trust. They have been given glimpses of the truth—but only glimpses.

Wordsmouth would have his fellow humans believe that our Father is a taskmaster—a slaveholder—or possibly a creator of robots! Of course your young minister is angry! Of course God is angry! We are angry too. And

Wordsmouth is getting very close to blasphemy. It would be well for you to help your young minister to better understand our Father's purpose in Creation. Possibly my experience can help you. Let me tell you a story:

Once on the earth, there was a little boy who was very lonely. He had no playmates. His human parents gave him everything to try to make him happy. They gave him a great room and told him that he could have every toy that he wanted for the room. He decided that he would build an elaborate electric train. He had tracks going in every direction. There were dozens of engines and passenger cars and freight cars. There were bridges and towns, rivers and roads. Little mechanical people walked on the streets, lived in houses, and rode in the trains. Each day, new toys and parts were added. Soon the room was full! But the boy was not happy. He was proud of his accomplishments, but there was no one to whom to show them.

The little boy complained to his parents, and they built him another game room—and another. But he was bored with his elaborate and lonely rooms. He was very unhappy . . . end of story.

You see Angelique, machines give nothing back. They do not have the qualifications of being alive, of being individual, of having intelligence, and of being free—of having a soul.

Humans play with their toys when they are children. They grow up to adulthood and continue to play with new toys. They call them automobiles and computers and businesses and nations. Some humans even believe that other humans are nothing more than toys.

Our Father has not made an elaborate electric train. He has made souls, and He has made them alive, individual, intelligent, and free. And He has given of Himself in this creation.

The gift of freedom is no pretense. Some humans, like Wordsmouth, have suggested that there is only the appearance of freedom: that in fact God has predetermined all things with His power and knowledge and presence, and His plan was completed from the start. Rubbish! Can Wordsmouth not see that such a creation would be like the little boy's train room? No harm would be done to the trains by such a suggestion. Trains are machines. The God of all creation is very different from a builder of machines. To call God a builder of machines is to deny the goodness of God's loving plan. To suggest that God has predetermined everything from the start is to deny freedom. His plan to create the soul would be thwarted. Creation would be incomplete. It would not be the glory. God has the qualities of omnipotence, omniscience, and omnipresence, of course. However, in creating the soul, He chose to limit Himself—to give a part of these away—in order to make the soul free. Thus the soul is made from a part of God. This gift of soul has boundaries, but within the boundaries there is real life, real individuality, real intelligence, and real freedom.

When our Father created the soul, He also created a world where the soul could exercise its gifts of life, individuality, intelligence, and freedom. In that world the choices must be real: choices between good and evil, fair and unfair, commitment or lack of it; bad, worse, maybe, fear, indecision, not knowing, faith . . . and the train tracks cannot all eventually lead to Heaven. If Heaven were automatic, then the soul would be un-free, and God's purpose would be thwarted. God's Heaven would be only another train room.

In the world the precarious must exist. Life must face death. Plans must face possible accidents. There must exist pain for pleasure, sickness for health; hurricane, tornado, flood, cancer, earthquake, disaster; or else the tracks would all lead to Heaven. God would have His soul back again—automatically—like an electric train.

There must be Hell, and it must be attractive. If the soul does not face Hell—and want it—and choose to leave it for something better, then the soul cannot know Heaven. And the choice must be on faith alone, not seeing clearly the reward. Passions, abused, can and will destroy. Yet passions lure all souls. Love without commitment—pure passion which is every human's fantasy—looks good, and it must! The soul must learn that only love with commitment brings joy. It is the joy of fellowship. And the soul must choose it.

Real fellowship can exist only where real freedom exists. Fellowship is a relationship of souls. The souls must be alive, individual, intelligent, and free; but also, for fellowship, in at least some ways equal: the equality not of talent or power or wealth, but of quality of life, of essence, of nature. Our Father is our parent. Souls are children who sometimes take their inheritance and squander it. The Christ gives an example in His Prodigal Son story. But the Father still wants those souls for fellowship—for Himself. All good parents want each of their children to grow up to be whole, to be adult, and to be their friend. Our Father wants that for human souls. We angels know. Humans will know.

But remember! God has taken a great risk! There is always the possibility that the child, if given freedom, may never be the parent's friend. Indeed, the child may become an enemy. And so, Hell or turning from God, is ever the human possibility—an eternal possibility. That is our Father's risk in creating the soul . . . alive, individual, intelligent, and free. The soul may reject the fellowship—with other souls—and with God!

However, Angelique, I would not have you forget the Divine Hope. Our Father's love is the most powerful force in the universe. We believe that He will one day win all souls unto Himself. Creation is not finished, if one soul remains in Hell!

With Divine Hope—
Your Loving Uncle Gabe

IV

THE UNITED WAY

Dear Angelique,

Yes, it is a great tragedy to see an intelligent, attractive spokesman for our Father, such as Dr. Tunnel, following his theological fallacies into a corner; then discovering so many friends in the same corner, that even if he could see the way, he would not come out; because he has found it comfortable there. The corner is our enemy's trap, of course, and he uses it for great destruction.

Dr. Tunnel was a fine minister. He has known our Father's love and has been given many gifts of the spirit. His human friends call him "charismatic," because of his appealing appearance and sincere personality.

Recently he broke with his congregation and took those members who supported him and organized a new congregation. He felt that the older congregation was not properly following his pastoral leadership. The incident left the older congregation sadly weakened.

More recently he has called his new congregation to withhold their financial support from the unified institutions of charity in his city, because he disagrees with the purpose and activities of one of those institutions. The objectionable group is called The Relationships Committee. It is one of our Father's favorite charities, deeply involved in ministering to human suffering in an area of great controversy.

The idea of withheld financial support is unbelievably bad, and the shock waves from the glee in Hell have been felt among the hosts! Just think, if Dr. Tunnel and his followers succeeded, not only would The Relationships Committee be abolished, but dozens of other charities which care for orphans, the feeble, the sick, the lonely, and the lost . . . all would be seriously hurt or destroyed.

You see, Dr. Tunnel believes in absolutes. That, at least, is what he calls them . . . "Absolutes." We of the hosts believe in absolutes. *GOD IS THE ABSOLUTE.* To believe in absolutes is good and true. But Dr. Tunnel has selected certain ideas—ideas that are generally good ideas—or good principles—but which are by no means absolutes. He has called them "Absolutes," and has allowed these ideas to lead him into his philosophical corner. Because he believes these ideas to be absolutes, he believes that they must not be compromised. Even allowing differing ideas to exist would be a compromise in his eyes. Therefore, differing ideas must be destroyed! The whole point of view becomes a way of life, and everything is seen then as black and white, good or bad, right or wrong.

The truth is God has created a world for humans where in every moment of their lives they are faced with hundreds of decisions. None of these decisions are absolutely right or wrong—just many shades on a spectrum between right and wrong. The Relationships Committee is very much aware of the spectrum and has courageously attacked a serious and controversial (among humans) area of human suffering. No such human organization does everything perfectly. Humans make mistakes. But the work of the Relationships Committee is in the direction of our Father, and His blessings are upon their ministry.

Dr. Tunnel sees the work of the Relationships Committee as evil, because some of their solutions to human problems appear to be "bad." He does not consider the fact that there are no better alternative solutions; or at least there are none available to the Relationships Committee and the people with whom they work. From his point of view, if solutions are imperfect, they are "absolutely" bad and must be destroyed, regardless of the cost—even if the cost is the destruction of Christ's Church.

Dr. Tunnel, if successful, would eventually find himself in Hell, surrounded by egotistical, self-serving devils, and think that he had established a new church!

Angelique, let me try to explain Dr. Tunnel's thinking, which allows for his point of view and leads him and many others into his "corner."

Many humans believe that our Father loves only a few. They see sin and evil in the world—indeed in themselves—and cannot understand a God who loves all. Their understanding suggests a completely holy God, so pure that He cannot look upon sin. He must love only a few: the chosen . . . the elect who have His blessing, His salvation.

Since humans cannot bear to be outside of a sense of God's blessing, the rationalization follows that surely their group is the "few" which He loves. They establish a set of rules which they call divine, obey these rules themselves, and demand that these are God's rules. Then they insist that these rules constitute the only way to salvation; and all humans are damned unless they join this group, follow these rules, and accept this plan.

The next step in this system of thought is the view that the world is corrupt and evil. God made it good, but it has gone bad. Humans must wash their hands of it, as God has, separate themselves from it, and find their salvation through the one true group which has God's rules.

Usually the group has a savior, and the savior is seen as divine. Many of these groups see the Christ as their savior and ironically portray Him as the sweet, loving one who saves them from God's wrath by taking on their sins and dying for them. Christ is understood by them as the defender against God's holy wrath. Christ, though divine, is at odds with God!

Such is Dr. Tunnel's belief. As you can see, it comes so close to the truth! But it is not the truth, because it fails in its first step to understand our Father's love. His love is the absolute! His love is complete. His love is full. His love is perfect. His love is eternal. God is love!

Our Father does not love only a portion of His creation. He loves all. He does not love only a few humans. He loves all. He counts the hairs on their heads. Their sin is their abuse of their greatest blessing: God's gift of His own spirit in their souls: that their souls are free!

Our Father understands sin. He understands that if left unchecked in the human soul, it will greatly damage that soul. He understands that the freedom He has given means that each soul has the right to choose sinful ways and can choose to have Hell eternally. And He understands the full tragedy of Hell.

But human sin does not change our Father's love of the human soul. Our Father has been loving all humans and revealing Himself to them in differing ways, in all places, in all ages, throughout all human history. That is a part of what the human soul is: one visited by God. The differences in human faiths, religions, and religious beliefs are the result of differing abilities and willingnesses to see and understand and absorb the revelations. The Christ is our Father, Himself, showing His love; not a son at odds with his father.

Dr. Tunnel can withdraw his support from unified charities when he disagrees with a small part, because the small part represents an absolute evil for him. He is trapped by the fallacy of his position and feels that he must remain loyal to the fallacy. The irony is that he does not even see that it is a fallacy. It will require deep soul-searching to the roots of his faith for Dr. Tunnel to return to an understanding of our Father's mercy and His love for all, not just a few, of humankind.

In Him because He loves us,
Uncle Gabe

V

TWO JUDGES: JUSTICE AND MERCY

Dear Angelique,

I must tell you about two humans who appeared here from the earth planet recently. On the earth-planet they were called "judges" (though we in celestial circles know, of course, that there is but one "Judge"). The end of their earthly lives had come on the same day, and with rejoicing we received them at the heavenly gates. Peter welcomed them as you know he does all humans who desire the heavenly fellowship. Their cases were rather unique, and so I relate them to you for your edification.

The first human, called Judge Fairvue, was truly a just man. He had been presiding in a human criminal court for twenty-nine years. During his professional career he devoted his life to the study of fairness, equality, and justice. He was a scholar in human law. As a human judge, he was a man of high integrity, always with a concern for the humans of his earth-town; their welfare and their safety. But he tried to be fair to the human criminals (those whom he found guilty of disobeying human requirements of responsibility to each other). He made a point of never giving punishment more severe than his understanding of their crime.

Judge Fairvue had carefully guarded against all of the meanness, vengefulness, corruption, and abuse of his power which are the enemy's usual weapons of temptation for humans of his position. By his understanding of human justice, he was just. And he gladly entered into our fellowship here. Our choirs sang a special "Amen" at his reception.

The second human, Judge Carejust, was very different. He, too, had been a scholar in human law and had devoted his life to the pursuit of justice and fairness. But we had to request of him that he go to the enemy, below, and so he is now in Hell.

You see, he had a completely differently understanding of justice. He did not define justice as fairness or equality. His understanding of justice was that it proceeds from mercy. He believed that his task as human "judge" meant that he must truly care about the souls of the criminals—as well as the souls of the victims of their crimes. He was a man of extreme self-discipline. He rigorously studied the causes of the crimes both in the lives of the criminals and in the world which surrounded them. He learned of their families and the families' needs.

Sometimes Judge Carejust's sentences of punishment were more severe than Judge Fairvue's—sometimes less. But his judgments were always based upon an attempt to help the criminal in the long run. While a criminal was in prison, he sought help for the criminal's family, inviting family members to his home and being a friend to them. When the criminal's punishment was completed, he helped the ex-criminal find work and new friends. He helped him or her learn to trust people again. He believed that our Father loves criminals, and that he must not stop loving them. He saw them as brothers and sisters.

He was a rare human. Our Father had use for his very unusual qualifications—his understanding of justice as mercy and his personal compassion. Therefore God asked that he continue to use these qualifications in that "well of untrust" where so little mercy is known. As you know, he will not be alone there. We have many others. Even the blessed Son has spent much time there.

Ah, but some souls are so mean or weak . . . and others are so stubborn . . . and others, yet, so blind. But our Father never gives up on any soul, and He needs the help of all souls who understand mercy. Judge Carejust seemed quite surprised and very excited about his new assignment.

And that brings me to the reason for my telling you of these two judges. Most humans have so much trouble believing in our Father's complete love! Though the Christ told them over and over—of how God is like the father of prodigals, that He *is* love, and that His love is eternal—humans still do not believe. They see their pain and suffering as forebodings of our Father's wrath, when in truth pain and suffering are but parts of His discipline to lead them to light and life. They think that their punishment is a permanent anger of God, when usually it is self-inflicted and temporary. They can not believe that God desires all souls and that Creation itself is the expression of His love.

Judge Fairvue is a human of whom we are very proud. His is fine and good in every way. But Judge Carejust has discovered the heart of God! Your young minister has been given visions of our Father's love and seems to have the beginnings of an understanding of God's heart. Cultivate his mercy and forgiveness and compassion. They are the possessions which he receives directly from our Father.

Affectionately,
Uncle Gabe

VI

ECUMENISM

Dear Angelique,

No, you would never have graduated from Angel College if your
spirit had not been true on ecumenism. Your writing to me,
questioning your own feelings, proves the dangers we risk when we send
out our guardians. Sin and evil can be so subtle that even our best angels
need refresher courses and nurturing. Remember, you are in constant
contact with our Hosts, here. How much more difficult it is for humans,
who know only by faith! And so we must continue to lift up those things
which nourish their faith: the disciplines of which we shall speak in later
letters—the spiritual disciplines for the full life.

You were right to seek help. You have been sent to a particularly difficult
area of the earth, where there are so many differing "Christian" beliefs. (I
believe they call it the "Bible Belt." It is apparently where they are "belting"
each other with their Bibles!) Some very bad ideas are being passed around
in the name of Christianity—ideas which oppose the very purpose of the
Christ.

One bad idea is that there is a certain group of humans who have a right
to consider themselves the *only* church: a chosen few who have an exclusive
right to our Father's love. There are many human groups in your area that
believe this about themselves. And they are able to convince themselves that
all other are wrong—doomed to some kind of eternal damnation which is
itself a creation of their own bitter imaginings.

Most of these exclusivist groups are made up of very good humans,
but they come together out of fear. They fear our Father's love because they

perceive it as an extremely limited love. They fear God's created world. They fear life. They fear death. Indeed, they fear God! Their concept of God is often that He is a tyrant who doles out severe punishment to anyone who even slightly displeases Him. As is normal for humans, they have feelings of hate. But they believe that their own hate is a reflection of God. Since their tyrant god hates his enemies, they live in constant fear that they may be seen by God as His enemies. They are never sure that God loves them. Thus, they fear eternity. (It is interesting to note that this fear-thinking makes them believe that hate is acceptable! Satan is delighted!)

Their fear drives them to seek answers and security, and they turn to the Bible. In the Bible they look for something that will make their group distinct: something that will separate them from the world which they fear and the people whom they dislike and distrust. And so they investigate the scriptures, seeking an idea, a passage dealing with some aspect of religion which other humans have missed. They pick an idea, but the idea they pick is usually insignificant, though often having to do with some aspect of Jesus' earthly life.

Imagine that Jesus one day was dipping soup from a large pot and noticed that the pot was cracked. Noting the crack, he might have suggested that he knew some people like that—that some people couldn't hold the truth in their minds, even if it were made perfectly clear to them. He then repaired the crack.

The exclusivists would then pick up on the story and glorify the idea of the redeemed pot—a miracle! The idea then would be lifted up to be crucial, absolute, and essential. A religion could be developed around the idea, with an organization and definite rules. They might call themselves the Holy Society of Redeemed Cracked Pots for Christ! This organization and these rules would become for them the source of salvation (their hope of eternal life with God), the sole source of salvation. All humans who do not join their group are surely damned. They could get salvation if they wanted it. All they would have to do is join their "church" and believe the "right things."

Such religion, as you well know, Angelique, makes a mockery of truth. When it is taken seriously, it is our enemy's favorite guise.

Truth is open. Truth is inclusive. Truth loves life and leads humans bravely into life's midst. Truth fears no death, because it has conquered death. And truth does not fear eternity, because it knows that eternity is the mountain of our Father's goodness. Truth is God.

Many humans have found our Father's truth, and it has led them into building fellowships of care and concern and compassion. Such fellowships seek out other groups that have found the same truth. And though they have different names around the earth, they recognize each other and seek to work together, because they know and understand love. Love unifies and love creates cooperation. Loving humans see human suffering, and wherever it is, in whatever form it appears—hunger, sickness, loneliness, lostness, greed, ignorance, selfishness, fear, hate, oppression, or any other form of suffering—these loving humans join their hearts and their fellowships together to deal with the suffering.

The fear groups and their frightened humans never seem to understand the love fellowships. If God is hard and cruel, as they believe, and loves only them, then these other groups who join together in "ecumenical" loving associations are of all people most suspicious. They must be stopped! After all, they are lost souls caring about and associating with Godless sufferers. In the eyes of the fear groups, ecumenism or cooperation is the result of the compromising of conviction and principle. It matters not that their own conviction is little and narrow, and their principle is insignificant! Ecumenism is seen by them as the Devil's workshop.

Angelique, your feelings are true. Ecumenism is our Father's way. One day all humans will put away their fears and suspicions and their selfishness, and venture out into our Father's beautiful creation and establish one ecumenical Church for the whole world. This Church will include the entire human race, and each human will respect every other human's beliefs and religious traditions and yet be of one Church. Then all humans will know our Father's truth which is His love—and God's Kingdom will come on earth as it is in Heaven.

Trustingly,
Uncle Gabe

VII

DAZED RIGHTEOUSNESS &
DISTURBED CHURCH MEMBERS

Dear Angelique,

So you are frustrated and confused already! I am not surprised. Suddenly you find that your young minister is in serious trouble . . . all because he has attempted to be creative in his ministerial work.

His appointment to the Riverville Church was disappointing. The Riverville Church is really too small to keep a minister busy. It ought to be rejoined to a circuit of churches—possibly a team ministry parish. But one of the enemy's tactics, several decades ago, was the implanting of a misdirected ambition among the ministers: that all churches should be single churches . . . that somehow circuit parishes were less prestigious and beneath the dignity of the "trained" clergy. This misdirected ambition was endowed by the enemy with a severe contagion that infected first the bishops, superintendents, elders, and deacons, and then the members of the congregations. Consequently, the members think that they must have their own pastor, regardless of the fact that they cannot support a pastor; and the Riverville Church, like many other little churches has become a proud but dying church. The enemy's plan is the carefully calculated spiritual death of young ministers and their churches.

Your young minister is alert to this problem and is attempting to be creative in his ministry. His present problem is related directly to this creativity. He was able to perceive that to build our church in Riverville, he must, among his other duties, minister to the young. When I heard that he was helping with music in the school and developing a youth club on week-end evenings and planning exciting programs and events for the young people—and, more important, getting to know and understand the youths personally—I was very pleased. Your advice and persuasion were admirable, my nephew.

Ah, but you forgot to keep up your guard against the enemy. He has such devious ways, perfected through the ages, of turning our work against us. If we are not careful, he slips up on us without our knowing.

You see, while your young minister was building the youth program, he also was preparing and preaching Sunday sermons on very controversial issues. His sermons were centered on our Father's love for *all* people—all races, all religions, all classes. Thanks to the work of the enemy among the church members, subtly promoting his powers of hate and prejudice, such preaching is not appreciated. The leaders of the congregation had warned him against such preaching, informing him that they wanted sermons that would make them feel good, not "stir them up" about people that were no concern of theirs—people who were "different" from themselves. But he, and you, my nephew, heeded not their warning (of course, we give thanks for you). And the sermons came rather close to being our Father's Word!

Many church members are not ready to hear our Father's Word. Oh, they need to hear it. You must use your best resources to help your young minister to continue preaching it! But the members have reacted strongly, and the different members have developed differing ways of reacting.

There are those who hear the true Word and, with the enemy's influence, develop a very acute deafness. I call it "dazed righteousness."

Dazed righteousness is an affliction characterized by a peculiar ability to hear *true preaching*, agree with it, even cheer it on; but then set it aside into a little compartment where it has no effect on life or decisions or activities. Infected with this affliction, such church members are not disturbed as they should be by true preaching. Their deafness is like being spiritually asleep! The ethical apathy among these church people is such a serious problem that we have developed a special school to train our guardians to deal with it . . . to restore church members' hearing ability! There is great potential for good among these members.

There are problems with other church members—very different from the problems of those afflicted with "dazed righteousness." They are very disturbed by true preaching. It points out to them conflicts between the Christian Faith and their lifestyles! Many of these members separate themselves from others and consider themselves a superior race and members of the only true religion. They want to be thought of as the "cultured" and "elite" of Riverville. The church is their country club. Do not expect them to like your young minister's preaching. He is suggesting that they should be loving their neighbors, regardless of race, religion, "culture," or economic status. And do not expect them to like the idea of associating with the poor, or, more to the point, having their children associate with the poor. These members are the ones who are causing the real trouble for your young minister.

While your young minister has been busy building a youth ministry and preaching the Word, these disturbed members of the congregation have been busy talking among themselves and complaining to the church officials who are his superiors.

We are really very nearly helpless, here, at the present. Our technique— indeed, God's plan—is that humans be free. This freedom allows them to do good or evil. Some will support your young minister in his creative ministry, helping the church to be an instrument for good in Riverville (and *good* will prevail—in our Father's *good* time). Others will fight any change or creativity that threatens their personal, self-centered, "country club" church. Our best angels are ever present trying to help those who shut our Father out, surrounding them with His love. But humans must remain always free to choose.

It is difficult to advise you, my nephew, in your guardianship when your young minister is having these problems with some of his parishioners and his earthly superiors. The problems are very complex, and I see a great deal of pain ahead for the young minister and you.

You must encourage him to be true to his faith and uphold his integrity at all cost. Otherwise we will lose him to the enemy. Possibly your best approach in this matter is to remind him that pain is a mysterious part of our Father's purpose for him and for all humans who are growing and living. Remind him that we, too, suffer, as our Father suffers. Remind him of the cross. Remind him, that without pain, there is no creation, no growth, no conquest over the enemy and his forces of death and darkness. Remind him that there is great work to be done in Riverville. We will be with him, but the work will not be accomplished without pain.

My blessings upon you,
Uncle Gabriel

VIII

PUBLIC RELATIONS

Dear Angelique,

I am so pleased that you appreciated my last letter. I was distressed to tell you of the future for you and your young minister. But you are one of our earthly bright spots, and all of us here send our great love and admiration.

Yes, I will be happy to tell you about Superintendent Slightly and Bishop Tack. They both have been of concern to us, for in many areas of the earthly church, we are making great progress. (There is a spirit of unity and good will spreading over the land like a warm summer breeze, and people are talking of bringing together the various divisions of our Christ's earthly body, the Church.) But in your area, there is little progress. Indeed, we are fearful that we are losing earth rapidly there, in part because of the influence of these two church officials.

Superintendent Slightly has fine qualities of warmth and leadership. His problem at first was simply the desire to be successful and well-liked. It was easy for the enemy to send Twistflesh to win him. Twistflesh has been specially trained to turn harmless ambition into helpless servitude to the enemy. The simple process gives easy rewards of success and popularity in return for slight compromises of integrity. The small half-truths are gradually turned to huge lies, but the process is carefully concealed from the victim, and often he feels quite self-righteous, because he is working for a "larger" goal. Beautimus, our guardian to Mr. Slightly, held up integrity and all of the great truths before him, but success and popularity looked too good to him. I am afraid that we have lost him—at least temporarily.

We also have our problems with Bishop Tack. Ceritas, his special guardian, is one of my best angels. Ceritas has reported regularly to me, and so I am familiar with the bishop's problems. The bishop began his ministry with many fine qualities. He had a naturally liberal spirit—open to new ideas and unafraid of change. He had considerable intelligence and a rather high devotion to honesty. He got along well with people, too. He seemed to like them. A pleasant personality is a very good thing for us, you know. As a matter of fact, for several years we thought that he would be one of our great spokespersons. He had such fine potential.

I am afraid that I must accept some of the blame for our loss of the bishop. In my enthusiasm for him, I simply did not see his weakness. It is an old weakness that has appeared many times in history—but never with the dangers that we see today.

His weakness has been an inability to see that *individual persons* are our Father's real concern. Nothing in all creation is more important to God than one single, individual soul. In his early ministry, Bishop Tack's enthusiasm for the Church effectively covered this weakness, this blind spot. The blind spot was picked up by Thumbhand, one of the enemy's best devils, and we were caught off guard. The bishop's easy rationalization—that the Church, the very body of Christ, is our Father's instrument for humans, and that it must be built at all cost—seemed to be a constructive rationalization.

But very soon we learned that "at all cost" included stepping on and all over people. At first they were hard and obstinate people who needed some "stepping on" for their own good. But Thumbhand was shrewd (they always are shrewd). He clouded issues and confused Bishop Tack so that he began to fail to distinguish between people and objects. In the bishop's eyes, human souls ceased to be souls and became objects. "Build the Church" was his motto—at all cost! And many good humans who got in his way suffered.

And then the young Tack found a new philosophy. I am sure that Thumbhand was responsible (though we never knew when it happened). I believe that the philosophy is called "public relations" in the world (we have no such concept in Heaven, and so it is a philosophy very difficult for me to grasp). As I understand it, the basic idea is that when people "get along" with each other, good things happen. Then, "getting along" becomes the primary function of life. To build the Church, it is a very useful philosophy, because it is true that when things are pleasant in an organization, that organization tends to grow in numbers.

The word "image" has become an important word in the philosophy. Whereas previously it simply meant "reflection" as in a pool of water, now it seems to have the connotation of "mask" or "costume," making individuals who wear it appear different from what they are. Thus, this "public relations" philosophy gives individuals and organizations public "images" so that their true identity is hidden from the public.

I am sure that you know that many businesses are using the "public relations" philosophy. It also has entered the political arena. We hear that the enemy is delighted that the use of this philosophy has become a threat to free elections in the democratic countries. Even thieves and scoundrels can hide easily in "images" (the old terminology was "wolf in sheep's clothing"). A new profession called "advertising" has developed around the concept of "image making."

It is no surprise to find the philosophy at work in the Church. After all what is good for business must be good for the Church! (Ah! I must apologize—even I stoop to the enemy's form of humor sometimes.)

Bishop Tack fell for it, hook, line, and sinker. He lost his ability to distinguish between public relations and Jesus' teaching that we love one another. He could not see that "getting along" with each other is quite different from loving one another; or that when "getting along" becomes the primary function of life, the virtues of truth, courage, hope, fidelity, faith, and love all suffer.

"Getting along" must be the result, not the primary purpose of the good life. As you well know, we get along with each other quite well in Heaven. But it is because we love each other, not because we want to use pleasantness as a way of achieving personal success. Even the enemy's troops "get along" very well in Hell (if they don't, they are punished). It is clear that "getting along" and "loving" are quite different.

After Bishop Tack traded "loving" for "getting along," he then mistook "building the Church" for "increasing in numbers." He has forgotten the concept of our Father's remnant in the Old Testament, or that Jesus' immediate ministry was with only twelve. Our Father speaks to people in gatherings large and small, but usually small.

Thus, a simple weakness in the bishop, the inability to understand that our Father's primary concern is for individual people, developed into a cold and calculating business of budgets, reports, committees, and secret meetings; and they became his "Church."

My nephew, you must encourage your young minister to continue preaching our Father's Word of truth, courage, hope, fidelity, faith, and love. Help him to remember that all of the great virtues are good only as they are a part of our Father's love; that His love caused Him to create; that His love caused Him to choose a people; that His love was His message through His prophets and His Son; that His love is the only reason for a cross; and that in His love, He needs humans who will accept that cross.

Do not let your young minister fall for "public relations." He must continue to distinguish between "getting along" and sacrificially loving.

You are constantly a part of our
prayers and our hopes,
Uncle Gabriel

IX

REVERSE IDOLATRY

Dear Angelique,

You certainly are in an interesting predicament, now! Don't worry—remember, it will be all right. Your close association with humans causes you to forget our Father's view.

You say that your young minister has fallen in love with the church, more particularly his "denomination," and that at first you were pleased with this development, even encouraged it; but that now you are worried, because his heart has strangely hardened during this experience. Now you are trying to convince him that the church is not everything. Are you really surprised at your fellow guardians for being anxious about your actions?

But you are right, and I am very pleased at your perceptiveness. I only hope that you can pass on your insight to your human.

Your young minister has caught the disease known in stratospheric circles as "reverse idolatry." Idolatry, as you learned in elementary angelology, is the state when creatures love someone or something more than they love God. (We, too, are creatures!) All idolatry is dangerous, but "reverse idolatry" is especially dangerous.

There are very subtle forms of idolatry (Gruelgust is a master of subtleties) created by our attraction to things that in themselves are very good, yet not God. For instance, humans make an idol of the Bible—the book which contains our Father's Word—ah, I must devote an entire epistle on this matter in the future. They make idols of every great gift given them by our Father.

"Reverse idolatry" is a form of idolatry that relates to the Church. It is most interesting and very complicated. To understand it, we must remember that our Father has commanded humans to love each other (the most abused of all His commandments). Well, the Church is humans: originally those very special humans who have opened their lives to God's gift of grace.

It is very easy for humans to assume that to love the Church fulfills the commandment to love each other. But it is not the same. The commandment to love each other is a matter of an individual loving an individual. It is a matter of the soul. It is the divine spark in humanity. It is always one on one and face to face. To love the Church—an institution, a *collection* of humans—is to run the risk of being idolatrous, and it misses the essential.

Another side of this strange disease is that humans, in their incompleteness, must have an example. They learn to love only because our Father first loved them. Their chief example has been, of course, the Christ. Many souls have learned through Him that they should love as our Father loves.

Humans are taught to worship our Father. But even we of the high hosts often forget that God, too, worships. Oh, not as we do! We must worship. Our nature, like the human's, requires that we worship or our souls wither as a leaf plucked from its branch. We simply cannot survive without contact with our creator. But God's nature is complete. He needs nothing. And yet (and I have this from the highest sources and have observed it myself), He does seem to have a need, by His very nature, to love—to have an object for His love. Some believe that this is why God began creating. In any event, strange as it seems, God really has great affection for humans—so great that it almost seems that He worships them (oh, the pain it must cause Him).

Our Father created the Church. It has been called the continuing body of His Son. Yet for Him to love "the Church" above the divine spark—the soul—the individual person—would be for Him idolatry.

Now, do you begin to see the meaning of the term, "reverse idolatry?" Humans must love as God loves. God, too, loves His Church. But, the only saving love is face to face. If our Father placed the Church above humans, it would be for Him, idolatry, and that would be "reverse idolatry," God worshiping the Church—"reverse idolatry" because it would be God placing something above His love of human souls. (Regular idolatry is when humans place something above their love of God.) God's perfect love of course never allows idolatry or "reverse idolatry." But for humans, the problem is very subtle, often obscure, and very dangerous.

Humans fall into the trap of "reverse idolatry" by loving the Church more than each other or God. To love in any way other than face to face, even though the thing loved may be of itself good, is what we call "reverse idolatry." It is a form of very serious idolatry: terrible because it is so difficult to recognize. How does a guardian angel lead his human to understand that to worship something that is a gift of God—but not God—is still idolatry? It is a very difficult task! But we must use our strongest efforts in this task, because some of our best humans fall into this, our enemy's very dangerous trap. It is a trap that can lead to many other forms of evil, including the worst kinds of bureaucratic and dictatorial government.

My advice to you is to keep placing before your young minister Christ's first and second commandments,

"You shall love the Lord your God with all your heart, and with all your soul, and with all your strength, and with all your mind; and your neighbor as yourself." (Luke 10:27 RSV)

Remind him of the parable of the ninety and nine. And keep him reading John's epistle about whoever sees a brother's need and "shutteth up his bowels of compassion" from the brother, cannot be of our Father. (Those King James translators surely had a way with words, didn't they?)

With high respect,
Uncle Gabriel

X

THE IDOLATRY OF BIBLE WORSHIP

My Dear Angelique,

What a delightful story you tell! Oh, yes, I am sure that the situation has caused some alarm in Riverville; but really, it is the sort of problem that causes laughter in Heaven. We do love to see good humans disagree, because that is our Father's great plan for their growth.

Ho! Ho! Ho! Did old Mrs. Stopall really shout out in the middle of your minister's sermon? What a shock—people just don't shout out at preachers in their sermons—even in a Bible Belt church like Riverville!

Let me see if I have the story right . . . you say that during the sermon, your young minister was raising questions about the Bible. And he serves a church in the Bible Belt! Very few people dare to question the Bible in the Bible Belt! The Bible is God in the Bible Belt!

He stated that he did not believe that a particular verse in Psalm 137 was an expression of God's will. He, of course, was referring to that terrible verse about smashing babies on a rock.

It was then that Mrs. Stopall stood up in church and screamed, "If God didn't write the Psalms, who did?" Wonderful to behold! I wish I could have been there. Things must be happening in that church!

I'm with Mrs. Blessings. She is the real saint in that village. Encourage your young minister to keep a strong friendship with her. She can help him bring a little heaven to Riverville. You write that she jokingly said later, "You'd have thought that Mrs. Stopall knew that the psalmist wrote the Psalms!" I love it!

Yes, my nephew, I do think that your advice has been sound. Your young minister is absolutely right about that verse where the psalmist says that he who dashes Babylonian babies against a rock will be happy. It is no expression of our Father's will. Our Father loved the Babylonians even as He loved the Jews.

To understand that Psalm, one must realize that the psalmist's homeland had been conquered and destroyed by the Babylonians, and he was living as a slave in the distant land of Babylon, being mocked by his captors about His love for our Father. (The Babylonians had rejected our messengers almost completely at that time—you are too young to remember our troubles with them.) The psalmist simply confused his love for our Father with his own bitterness.

You have advised your young minister well concerning the nature of Scripture, but be very careful that he understands some important distinctions. Just because he is aware that human thoughts and emotions are at the heart of Scripture, he could easily forget that the true nature of these writings is that they contain our Father's eternal truths—His Holy Word. Many of our finest ministers have become aware of the humanness of Scripture, but then, in doing so, have lost a sense of the Divine. The result is an idolatry which worships goodness in humanity rather than truly worshiping our Father. There is goodness in humanity, and it is of God; but to worship anything but God is idolatry.

Our Father, in inspiring the writing of Scripture, has never violated the human will. He revealed Himself to the ancient writers just as He reveals Himself to people today, like your young minister. They caught great glimpses of Him and wrote about these experiences. Some saw our Father face to face—rare incidents of complete openness on the part of humans—incidents that have molded and changed earthly history. There was that openness among a few Jews in Palestine, and our Father took on human form and visited the earth planet to speak miraculously to that openness.

But never does our Father violate the human will. Even His favorites—I think of Simon Peter and Saul of Tarsus—remained always free and very, very human.

You must remember, my nephew, that humans want to believe in absolutes. Therefore they tend to make finite things into absolutes. They feel that they need absolute assurance. Yet, all that they really need is integrity, love, and a sense of purpose. God has withheld absolute assurance. It is a part of his plan to provide humans a road to Heaven . . . a road paved by their own choices. It is the road of faith.

The human desire for absolute assurance causes a second idolatry which is the direct opposite of the first (worshiping goodness in humans). The second goes so far as to deny goodness in humans; and Heaven knows that goodness has been implanted in them! It is the idolatry which mistakes a book, the Bible, for our Father, and thus worships it, not Him.

The Bible becomes the Word of our Father only when humans encounter our Father's Spirit in those writings, and only through those persons, who in the encounter allow His Spirit to work in them.

Remember, my nephew, that humans actually forget God's Spirit. Conceive of it! There is a blindness that begins to develop during early childhood. Young children rarely have trouble recognizing the Spirit. But as they grow older, humans can build their selfish walls around themselves so that they become blind to the Spirit, and they forget. Our Father planned for this possibility as the necessary result of human freedom and individuality. But in doing so, He allowed a great opening for the enemy.

Humans who have become blind to God's Spirit find it extremely difficult, if not impossible, to trust the Spirit's leadership. They cannot abide doubt. Doubt strikes fear into their lives. These humans consider doubt as the work of the devil, when in reality, of course, our Father's Spirit uses doubt to set them free, break down the walls of selfishness, and open their minds to His workings . . .

The Biblical writings tell of God's Spirit. But they often become used as if they were God, Himself. Those who fear doubt, who are blind to the Spirit, demand that all religion be confined in the pages of a book or in a set of rules. The Pharisees were such people in Jesus' day. They were good men who could not see the Spirit and did not trust our Father to lead their lives. The Son had great problems with the Pharisees.

Our Father inspired humans to write. He still inspires humans to write. His hope is that a message of love and trust is carried in the writings. Love and trust can open human lives to the reality of God's Spirit. Being open to God's Spirit is the beginning of true religion. It is faith.

For humans to require that the Bible be the infallible word of our Father is idolatry. Our father cannot be bound in any book. Imagine the small mind which would attempt it! Only the insecurity of spiritual blindness wishes it. The great Creator of the universe and the Sustainer of us all is always beyond anything which we can conceive or write. Even the inspired human mind can only begin to understand the vast glory of God. The concept of an infallible Bible is contrary to God. Satan himself would like, more than anyone, to contain God in a book!

Continue to encourage your human to prepare sermons showing humanness in Scripture . . . like in those terrible verses of the 137th Psalm. But also encourage him to see and proclaim the divine. His integrity in this area of preaching will create controversy around him. Uphold him in hard times.

Lovingly,
Uncle Gabriel

XI

EXPERIMENTING IN WORSHIP

Dear Angelique,

For quite a time I have been wanting to talk to you about human worship. Your excitement about your young minister's recent experiments with new forms of worship encouraged me to write to you. I am delighted that your young minister is "experimenting." It suggests an open and inquiring mind which frightens the pitchforks out of Hell!

You must remember that human worship is quite different from our worship. Humans are free to worship many things other than our Father, and they can worship in many ways. They may worship themselves, their possessions, power, money, and even the enemy. We are not free in the same sense, because we are committed. Oh, our Father has lost some angels—the enemy is the prime example—but only rarely. Our freedom is much fuller. It is the freedom of being in the presence of absolute love. You have known such fellowship. You have been to the Mountain where God is. You have *seen*!

Humans have not seen as we have seen. Their highest experience of our Father comes through their faith. Faith, for humans, is not seeing. Faith is not believing. It is so much more. Faith is trusting and letting life be directed by that trust. Humans' very limited fellowship with our Father is the most joyous experience that they can know. But their human hearts would burst if they *knew* our worship. The experience would be so overwhelming that the result would be the loss of their freedom. The divine purpose on earth is that humans have freedom so that they must choose to worship or not to worship our Father. (*That* is the question!)

We must, therefore, encourage their faith and insure their freedom. There are many matters about human worship which are important. Let me point out some of them to you:

First, you must help your young minister develop a proper perspective about tradition. Humans love traditions . . . sometimes too much. They even get traditions mixed up with God sometimes. But traditions are a good thing. Great and inspired humans have led worship in beautiful ways, when our Father and His choirs have felt very welcome. New generations of humans can learn a great deal from these "beautiful ways" which have been remembered and passed down through the earth-years. These "beautiful ways" become traditions.

The tragedy is when the new generations are taught that they are required to worship with the traditions of their ancestors. The old ways can become a substitute for God and actually block the possibility of worship. There is a great difference between listening to the angelic choir and being in it. Listening is a great thrill. Even we can be inspired as spectators. But to worship is *to be in the choir*—never just listening or watching, but singing!

Traditions are valuable aids in instruction and preservers of truth, but they must not be substituted for worship. Worship must be ever new. Worship must belong to the individual, the individual's day, and the individual's own group of worshipers. It must be the individual's offering to our Father.

Second, I have never known humans to worship without singing, if not with their voices, certainly with their hearts! Many humans attend worship and never open their minds or their hearts or their mouths in praise. They cannot know our Father. God does not care if they "carry" the tune. (One day He will give them voices which will ring out as Christmas Bells.) But if their hearts sing—if they love Him—they will praise Him. And one of the great gifts of our Father to humans is the ability to express themselves in music. Help your young minister to sing and to lead his congregation in singing.

You see, worship for humans is an expression of joy. The enemy, for ages, has been trying to shut that joy out. He cannot. One of our favorite sources of heavenly humor is that in spite of all of the enemy's threats, often from his deepest prisons, the divine spark (which is never put out, even in the most degraded human) shows itself, and songs of praise escape. On earth they are mistaken sometimes for earthquakes, but the truth is that those songs of praise frighten the enemy into a shattering stupor. (You can imagine his fear of a mutiny in Hell!)

My third point about human worship has to do with its effects. If real worship takes place—if forms are set aside and the individual soul and the gathered congregation meet our Father, face to face—if the creature meets the Creator, the experience is earth shaking! The human will never be the same again. Even if humans have the experience over and over again, each time they are changed. Each time they are cleansed. Each time they are made new. Each time they are strengthened. Each time they find themselves dissatisfied with the inferior life they had before.

You, my nephew, know that the same thing is true for us. When we travel to the Mountain where God is, we always grow to be more like God. So it is with humans. The effects are remarkable. In worship, if humans really meet God face to face, they are confronted with themselves. They see themselves clearly and know their own individual purpose and know that they must love more.

In worship, humans also are confronted with their neighbors. To meet God face to face necessarily causes humans to understand that God is the Parent of us all. Understanding the Parenthood, they know all humans as their brothers and sisters. No longer do they feel any shame about any of those with whom they associate. No longer do they feel the need to compete with them. No longer can they close their eyes to their problems and needs. Their own hearts and souls expand to such proportions that they know that, with our Father, they are all ministers, priests to each other, and that all humans are their parish.

With such an experience, the human performs acts that to others appear to be miracles. Humans change and whole cities change. It is a matter of grave sadness to us that *many congregations and many souls never experience true worship.*

Remind your young minister that if things are not ever changing in his church (only Heaven has the right to be satisfied with the status quo—and even Heaven is not!), then the highest forms of worship are not taking place. But if he can withstand the opposition—even enjoy it—and continue his experimentation, he will see the miracles!

Praise our Father,
Uncle Gabriel

XII

DENOMINATIONALISM

Dear Angelique,

I notice from your last letter that your young minister has been confronted with the full zeal of denominationalism. You say that one of the fine young men of his church has fallen in love with a lovely girl of another "persuasion," and wishes to marry her. She and he want to be members of both congregations, because they have relatives and friends in both. And, you say, they have invited your young minister and the other minister to share in the wedding ceremony in the chapel of her denomination.

Ah, youth is so innocent! Bless them! Yes, I know what happened, before you tell. The other minister would have none of it. He apologized but said he could not disregard denominational law. And your young minister said that he knew of no way for them to belong to both congregations, except by splitting their marriage. To complicate matters, the girl's denomination requires that she promise to raise all children in its beliefs; that if she does not, they will not accept her marriage as valid. If she goes to his congregation, her family will disown her. The boy must be re-baptized, attend classes on doctrine, and choose to be confirmed in her "persuasion."

The result is that the young Romeo and Juliet have decided to leave the Church completely and find a civil judge to marry them.

I know, I know. You, your young minister, the boy the girl, and even the other minister want to know how humans can call themselves our Father's Church when they allow the Church to be the instrument of dividing God's people, rather than uniting them!

I regret to tell that I have no immediate solution to offer you, or answer to give to the young couple. In their love, they are experiencing our Father more powerfully than is their divided Church with all of its doctrine. Our son, Martin Luther, served a great cause when he saw grievous injustices in the Church and stood against them. Ah, "the enemy below" fled before him. But when the enemy saw the divisions caused by the battle, he quickly came forward to use these divisions for his diabolic purpose. His success has been astounding. Our Church has been severed over four hundred times! And always there is talk of new divisions.

One of the forms of selfishness which our Father allows in humans (through His gift of free will—so that they can grow to their full stature as individuals) is the love of power. In the midst of controversy, humans easily rationalize that they, in standing for "the right," must divide. They persuade themselves that they must separate from those whom they believe to be wrong. In reality, many times if they used their energy loving each other in their disagreements (which is our Father's way), they would find their Church strengthened by their disagreements. Actually, their love of power, goaded by the enemy, causes them to divide. Their allegiance is not to the right but to their own selfish desire for power.

I do have news of exciting changes taking place on your planet. The warm breezes of unity in our Father are blowing across the land! On one populous little island, only a few years ago, two great denominations entered into conversations which were heard in the highest galaxies of Heaven. Communities found themselves worshiping and studying and serving together in ways they had not attempted for two hundred earth-years. I regret to mention that the enemy, with suggestions of "loyalty" and "apostolic succession" and "tradition," became firmly lodged in the lives of some of the denominational leaders. The conversations were halted for a time. But they will commence again! Such a spirit of unity cannot be checked!

Across the earth people from different denominations and even different religions are talking together and working together and exploring union. Many small mergers have already taken place. They know that they are working in our Father's will. We, in celestial circles, are excited. We know that it is coming! And we rejoice constantly to see the success that you and your other guardians are having as you remind your humans that our

Father's love always draws people together into loving communities. It always unites. It never divides.

I would suggest that your young minister meet again with the young couple and talk to them of the coming unity. Have him seek their patience and their help and their youthful enthusiasm—not to give up or run away. He might suggest that they visit other denominations—worship with them and discover one of the many that believes in tolerance and understanding as essential elements of God's way—where a celebration of human differences shows an understanding of God's will.

When they find such a denomination, suitable to both of them, help them understand that if they choose to join together, the joining must represent an equal sacrifice for each of them, so that there will never be the suggestion that they made a decision unfair to one or the other. There they will be able to raise their family in the unity of the Spirit.

Have your young minister ask the young couple to help him seek the unity of the Church.

Blessings
Uncle Gabe

XIII

COMPROMISE AND THE UNITY OF THE CHURCH

Dear Angelique,

For ages it has been a matter of great concern to me that so many humans oppose the unity of God's Church. I am pleased that you picked up on this point in my last letter. These opposers use selfishness, bigotry, and prejudicial arguments to support their divisiveness, pretending that it is for the good of the Church. Their arguments are pure rationalizations designed to support their personal prejudices.

The denominations do have theological and doctrinal differences, but in many cases it is because humans have created the differences to excuse the divisions. In other cases, the differences are only differing ways of expressing the same ideas. Humans who oppose unification say that to unite the denominations would require compromises of their theologies and doctrines. Compromises are seen as loss of conviction. Hence, the denominational leaders who oppose unity claim that unification will result in a weakening of the fiber of the whole Church—unity at the expense of character. Actually, these leaders have positions of power and prestige in their own denominations and are afraid they will lose their power in a unified Church. They would oppose unity even if it promised Heaven on earth, much less just the building of a stronger Church.

Strangely enough, these humans who oppose unification are right about one use of compromise. When compromise is used as a settlement for that which is less than right or less than true, it is wrong. Many times humans expect that good will prevail simply because it is good. But goodness is like creativity. It does not happen automatically. It happens when God and His people work for it. It is true that evil, bigotry, and ignorance never sleep. The enemy is constantly spinning his web. Humans are often caught in his web by attempting to use compromise in matters of righteousness and truth.

Many good humans have seen evil forces at work but have feared that to stand and fight would cause a great storm, resulting in more evil. They conclude that the only solution is to settle for a compromise, but such a solution is a compromise of the right and the truth. Such a compromise would have caused Moses to come to an agreement with the Pharaoh about slavery—though human slavery is always wrong—and would have caused the Christ to accept the Pharisee's legalistic religion to escape the cross. Throughout the history of earth and heaven, humans and angels have become our Father's messengers when they have refused to compromise righteousness and truth.

Let me remind you that right is love, and that truth is love, for God is love. Many humans become so self-absorbed that they forget that love is the source: it is God's nature. The source of righteousness is love, the source of truth is love, the source of faith is love, the source of power is love, the source of justice is love, and the source of all creation is love! It is too easy to reverse these thoughts and forget the source. As our son Paul wrote his letter about love to the humans in Corinth, the essence of our Father burst forth upon him and God's fullness was revealed . . . Calvary lived again. Paul understood God's true nature: that all of the creative forces of the universe are merely the expression of our Father giving Himself to His creation. Such is His love. And love calls forth unity, not diversity.

As for the particular argument of the denominational leaders who have opposed the unification of the Church, claiming that compromise weakens, I would say, some uses of compromise strengthen. These denominational leaders are letting their own lack of love and faith stop the work of the Spirit. They do not trust people who are different from themselves. In this case, their fear is directed toward members of other denominations, even though the others may be equally led by God. These leaders do not have faith enough to follow the Spirit of God into new paths of cooperation.

As I have said, the Spirit of God—His love—always unites, never divides. If by using compromise, a movement among the denominations creates respect and understanding and seeks unity, then it is of the Spirit of

God, and people of love and faith will recognize it. Compromise becomes a power for good when parties who differ come to realize that neither of their positions is entirely right or wrong . . . each has been seeing the good only from his or her own point of view. But the good is greater than any human point of view, and the good is strengthened, not weakened, by combining the two positions. A compromise represents that each is willing to give for the betterment of all. Compromise then becomes a useful and constructive step in following the will of God.

No human has a perfect theology. No earth denomination has a perfect doctrine. Whereas unification of the Church must never ask of humans that they be untrue to their concepts of God or be disloyal to their denominations, it does call for a higher loyalty. It calls for the love of God and the loving respect for all of His children. There is no reason under Heaven why all people cannot worship in one Church—even as they disagree in their human concepts. Differences of opinion, in love, cause growth. Honest debate, with respectful listening and the voicing of honest conviction, creates the atmosphere of growth.

Our Father's Church does not need exclusivist divisions for its life: denominations whose members think they are the only ones right with God. Our Father's Church needs cooperation. It needs humans who see the differences of their placements (humans call it race and gender and class and nationality and creed) and love each other and learn from each other by these blessed, God-given differences.

I am delighted that your minister is supporting the movement for unity in the Church. Keep close by his side. He will need you.

In the unity of the Spirit,
Uncle Gabriel

XIV

AUTHORITARIANISM

Dear Angelique,

Yes, I am deeply concerned about the state of the Church in your young minister's area. Your assessment of the problem is quite in line with the history we are keeping of the work. The Church has deteriorated greatly under the leadership of Bishop Tack, and there is great distress among the hosts. I can tell you now that your appointment to the area was made in the hope that you could be of help in dealing with a desperate situation.

In my letter to you about "Public Relations," I have given you some background on the bishop, so that you can understand how disappointed we are in him. The report which you have sent shows the natural result of leadership dedicated to nothing higher than how the Church "appears" to the public—not the truth about the condition of the Church as it faces its task of being God's instrument of compassion to the world and how it plans to accomplish that task. Unless there is a change of direction, many church leaders will trade their integrity for an "image." They will expect Christ's Church to move forward without ever grappling with human selfishness and their own abuse of power.

Christ's Church never moves forward without struggle. But these church leaders will come to dread openness and honesty and creative controversy. And as they do, they will lose their faith in God and in their fellow human beings. Proportionately, the Church will make its decisions out of fear, and it will act out of apathy and cowardice. Church members will begin to distrust each other. In the atmosphere of distrust, meetings will be held in secret, and the decisions reached in these meetings will be pronounced with authoritarian zeal. Authoritarianism will have taken the place of freedom, good leadership, sound judgment, and democratic procedure.

Within the authoritarian structure, favors will be handed out by the authoritarian leaders to those who are loyal to them and their system. Punishment rather than support will be given to those who are honest, and punishment to those who oppose the system because of their dedication to freedom, democracy, and equality for all of God's children. In the process, as success comes to those who obey the authoritarian leaders rather than to those of integrity, the atmosphere of distrust will increase, and tyranny will become "king" in the body of Christ . . . His Church!

Such is the possibility in your area, and your young minister has serious decisions to make. The hosts all wonder what will become of the Church, there. Even we in Heaven cannot see all of the future. However, never despair! We do know that if the Church dies, our Father will raise up new people and a new Church to do His work. Whether your young minister will be a part of the new or a part of the renewal of the old—or whether he will give in to the pressures around him—only he can decide. His freedom is real. We must encourage his faith and his creativity, so that he may find ever new ways of dealing with this problem of authoritarianism in God's Church.

The young minister's creativity can be inspired and encouraged by us and our guardians (like you). The inspiration may even come directly from our Father. Inspiration is a great gift from Him. However, choosing to be creative is the responsibility of your young minister. Just as human problems are real, so human choices are real, and the solutions resulting from those choices should be credited to them.

When humans pray, they align themselves to the power of God and His will, and the results cause humans to speak of miracles. They are not miracles from our point of view. They are just the results of humans allowing our Father's will to work through them. Our Father always answers their prayers (not always in the way they wish), but never by violating their freedom. His laws relating to human freedom are consistent in that He puts limits on their freedom, but He never forgets or takes away that freedom. Your young minister is really free to join the authoritarians and receive their favors—or to stand against them.

We hope your young minister will choose to align himself with the power of God. God's power always draws people together in loving fellowships dedicated to the marvelous qualities of freedom, democracy, and equality for all people. God's power is never on the side of authoritarianism. Authoritarian tyranny seeks to destroy the loving fellowships.

If your young minister chooses to stand against an authoritarian "takeover" of the Church in his area, he will be punished by the authoritarian leaders. But he will have aligned himself with the power of God which is eternal. In the total picture, it cannot fail!

Your task is to help. You are doing it well. I will write more on human creativity later.

All our love,
Uncle Gabriel

XV

HABITS OF THE FULL LIFE: DEVOTIONS

Dear Angelique,

Your letter was received with love. But I detect that you feel great alarm about your young minister. You are worried that he may be headed toward an experience of spiritual exhaustion. Such exhaustion can be the result of his using spiritual energy at a faster rate than he receives it. Spiritual energy is a gift from God—given in many ways. Humans often attempt tasks which are too great for them, using more spiritual energy than they receive. The result is often exhaustion or even breakdown. Humans sometimes call it a "nervous breakdown." Obviously, there are many causes for this human malady.

We of the celestial circles are delighted that on earth an infant science called "Psychology" is making important discoveries in the understanding of the human mind and spirit. It is one of the many ways science is being useful to people of the Church in their ministry of finding help for human problems.

I would like to suggest to you that there are certain spiritual necessities about which your young minister may not be aware. Humans must have a flow of spiritual energy into their lives daily, if life is to endure. Humans also have physical needs. It is simple to understand their need for fuel (food), air, shelter, etc. If their supply of food is taken away, their physical bodies quickly die. However, they usually do not realize that their spiritual nature is the same. They must receive regular spiritual fuel. To receive spiritual fuel with needed regularity, your human must follow certain **habits of the full life**.

First, humans must worship. I spoke in earlier letters about the human need for worship. And I have discussed the quality of worship with you. With regard to personal discipline, I speak now concerning a daily need for individual devotions and prayer . . . as well as the regular need for community worship.

The prophet Isaiah, a human who lived on your earth-planet seven hundred years before the Son's visit, had communications from God. He described beautifully the experience of meeting God. He, in a rare moment of openness, met God, face to face. Facing God always is, as you know, an overwhelming moment of joy. Think of what it must be like for humans, in the midst of their earthly limitations, to experience the eternal—in their physical limitations, to see Creation itself! That moment is a great experience of joy, but it is also very fearsome.

Many humans fall on their faces in awe. Many bend their knees and bow their heads in humility. They feel unclean in His presence. They know their incompleteness. They confess their sin. At the point of their uncleanness, their incompleteness, their sinfulness . . . God touches them and makes them whole. And their humanness is never quite the same. They hear His call. They want to serve Him. They want to love as He loves. They want to love their fellow humans as He loves His whole creation! Such was Isaiah's description of his experience of meeting God.

If your human wants the full life, he must seek this moment of openness each day. He needs to be a part of a community of worshippers. I often am amused at the Bible literalists on earth. They read the creation stories and think that our Father created the universe in six days and then rested. The seventh day (which conveniently comes four times each time the moon circles the earth, giving them a check for their calendar) became, earth-years ago, a celebration of our Father's rest day. What amuses me is to think that our Father created for six days and then ceased. God has never ceased! From the beginning, He has been creating and has never stopped. Humans cannot conceive of eternal creation, so do not expose your human to the idea too abruptly. But, it is the case!

Let me assure you that God does enjoy seventh-day celebrations! Seventh-day celebrations really meet the human need for community worship—for the community moment of openness. I only regret that humans have separated themselves from each other in so many ways. They rarely seek as communities, but rather as segments of communities. Yet even the segments can seek honestly and find our Father. Remember, Angelique, the Church's purpose is to proclaim the openness, not to contain it! My highest affection comes to you.

Sincerely,
Uncle Gabriel

XVI

FORGIVENESS

Dear Angelique,

I have watched with great interest the unfolding of events in Riverville with your young minister. I must admit that I am distressed at what you tell me, and I know that you are worried about his reactions.

Of course, he is upset! Of course, he is hurt. Of course, he has deep feelings of resentment toward Superintendent Slightlty and Bishop Tack. He was depending upon their support in his great project. He should have had their support, but they did not give it.

You see, my nephew, if your young minister had succeeded in establishing those new classes in the Riverville Church, it would have put an end to the dominance of Mrs. Stopall and her friends. They do not want the Riverville Church to be the Church! They want it to be their social club. Your young minister's ideas are too ambitious. What a wonderful thing it would be if he had been able to establish the class for the mentally ill and the class for the study of human prejudices. The class for troubled marriages was an especially fine idea. One of the great services which the Church can render to its community is the providing of opportunities for people to come face to face with their deepest troubles. In the Church, they can experience these opportunities among the people whom they know and trust and who face similar problems.

Your young minister's idea of developing such a school in his church was indeed exciting for a small town. It had the potential of introducing many new people to the Riverville Church, and its people would have been exposed to many new and wonderful possibilities for their lives.

But Mrs. Stopall and her friends would have lost their hold on "their" church. They could not allow such a loss of control. And so they convinced the officials to remove your young minister from Riverville.

Bishop Tack could see that the young man would be a threat to the normal methods of ministry, as well as a threat to the bishop's control of that ministry. He, therefore, has chastised your young minister severely and is sending him to another appointment.

I am very concerned about your young minister's feelings toward the bishop. It is a great shock to be deserted or betrayed—whatever the reasons. We can speak of forgiveness forever, but for a human to try to forgive the one who has betrayed him is a great test of love.

Remember the Christ at the time of his betrayal and trial. Even Peter denied him. Now we can look back and see Peter's remorse and understand that Christ's forgiveness of Peter was the result of their great friendship and love for each other. The fact that Peter became frightened and ran, after denying he even knew Jesus, was quite human. Jesus forgave him. We forgive him.

But the concept of total divine forgiveness is much more than just the forgiving of one friend by another—when one has disappointed or failed the other. Divine forgiveness is in the heart of the forgiver, and it is not dependent upon the situation or the cause. It is forgiveness, *because* it is love in the heart of the forgiver. It is complete and without reservation. It is the forgetting of the offense!

The forgiving of Judas by God is the great example. Everyone understands the forgiving of Peter. Everyone loves Peter. He was a good man who tried and failed. He was filled with remorse. He was forgiven.

Judas is another matter. Judas committed a wrong much more severe than denial. He not only denied, he betrayed. Jesus knew, understood, and forgave. Even for us in heaven, such forgiveness is truly the presence of God. But, for humans, such forgiveness is an unbelievable miracle! It is easy for humans to understand the forgiving of Peter, but very few humans can grasp the idea of the forgiving of Judas. One must truly understand the heart of God.

If you would lead your young minister in the ways of our Father, you must lead him in the way of forgiveness.

Love,
Uncle Gabriel

XVII

HABITS OF THE FULL LIFE: WORK

Dear Angelique,

Ah yes, my nephew! There is more to a daily discipline of personal habits than just the matters we discussed in our last letter concerning prayer and devotions. The constant turning of one's life to a consciousness of God is the foundation of the full life. But much must be built upon the foundation!

Your last letter included a host of new developments. I had heard of your young minister's disagreement with the bishop, and so I had expected the controversy to manifest itself in some way. It was no surprise that the bishop moved him from Riverville. I am glad that the young minister refused the appointment which the bishop presented him.

Ministers should stand for righteousness. They should be men and women of character and conviction. And the bishops and other leaders of the Church should encourage them when they exercise conviction. Thus the leaders can help create an atmosphere of freedom whereby the integrity of a courageous minister is supported. If the hierarchy of the Church fails the ministers in these times of struggle, then the Church has failed indeed.

We believe in humans. Our Father actually uses some of the essence of Himself when He creates them. The trouble is that so often humans do not believe in themselves or each other. Humans who are given positions of authority often treat their fellow humans as slaves to be mastered. The slaves are given no choices in the determination of their own work or futures.

The Church should be the example on earth of fairness and compassion. As we suggested in our letter to you about authoritarianism, our Father is not an authoritarian in His treatment of humans; therefore humans should not be authoritarian in their treatment of each other. Let decisions of the earth Church be made in the open forum of honest humans. Some earth Church denominations do not have in their organization the office of bishop. But in those that do, the office of bishop should protect the open forum. The primary purpose of a bishop is to be the minister to the ministers. The bishop does have other tasks which the complexities of his Church and society have placed upon him. It is good that his office carries with it the concept of ambassador of good will. It is good that he is often in a position to bring harmony, justice, and equality into torn human relationships. It is good that he can represent the Church, the Body of Christ, to many humans who have been denied the privilege of seeing the truth that the Church has to offer. But his first duty—indeed the only unique reason for his office—is to support and inspire the Church's men and women of the ministry. It should not be an office of authority, but an office of leadership.

And so your young minister is out of work. It will be temporary, I can assure you. But these will be difficult times. Your young minister has been trained to serve. Yet he holds no position of service. He has a wife and lovely children who look to him for support. Yet financial burdens seem to have no solutions. And most of all, he believes that he must work in order to be a whole person.

It is a shattering experience to the human ego to be jobless. He will be surrounded with feelings of defeat and failure. The enemy delights in such a predicament. If the enemy can instill some sweet bitterness into the heart of your young minister, some hate toward the human who put him in such a difficult time, your young minister will feel relief through his own bitterness. But the enemy himself will have become lodged as a cancer in the heart of your human. And major spiritual surgery will be required to dislodge such a hold by the enemy.

Encourage your young minister to anger. Encourage him to tears. Encourage him to laughter. But place your very spirit against his bitterness!

May I add this word about human daily discipline: Humans must work. They work or they die. Even if jobless—even if disabled—even if totally paralyzed, they must work. Our Father comes to them in their need and gives them work to do. The work may take the form of some service to a small corner of God's creation that the humans never before had seen. The work may be some new creativity in the individual human. That creativity might be some art, some study, some increase of the mind and understanding, some writing, some disciplining of the prayer life to lift the needy of the world to the throne of God. The work may come as the opportunity to love our Father in some new way.

The truth is that our Father has given every human a purpose: to grow. Growth requires work, and so, work must be a part of every human's daily discipline (angels, too!).

In His work,
Uncle Gabriel

XVIII

HABITS OF THE FULL LIFE: STUDY

Dear Angelique,

The news of your young minister's entry into the campus ministry warmed our hearts. One of the most neglected mission fields of the earthly Church is the college campus. It would seem that the Church is afraid of these centers of higher education. Yet marvelous things are happening in the colleges and universities. When men and women as students dedicate themselves to the seeking of truth, it brings them close to the throne of God. If God's creative purpose in humans is that they grow toward fellowship with Him, how suitable it is for them to have the search for truth at the center of their lives! Philosophers and scientists for centuries have lived under His special blessings—even when some of them have not recognized Him.

Into this magnificent atmosphere of seeking, questioning, and doubting—and finding, listening, and trusting—the students come. Even as they are overwhelmed with the intensity of their studies and endless assignments, it also is a time when they are faced with new difficulties and tough decisions for their lives. They are no longer children; they must make their own decisions rather than depend on their parents. They must wrestle with their understanding of purpose in life, and translate that understanding into a life's work—a career. They must deal with their sexuality: that glorious but very difficult gift from God which drives them to seek out a mate, to commit themselves to that mate—and love and be loved on a level similar to an experience of the Divine. (Indeed, when it is successful, it is God's preview of Heaven.)

These young students also must come, alone for the first time, to an understanding of their relationship with God. They are at that time in life when they need to develop a faith by which they can live with honesty and courage and unity of spirit. And they must prepare themselves for leadership and service in some future community where they will work, raise families, and, hopefully, serve our Father.

While decisions must be made, accelerating the maturing process to a frenzy, great pressures are thrust upon these students by teachers, parents, and classmates—causing them to forget the Church—indeed to rebel against it. The Church represents to them one of the pressures which would have them conform to traditional standards. Students do not want to conform, and so they rebel against the Church and God, little realizing that our Father is delighted with the rebellion. God creates each human to be different, and He intends that all find their individuality. He only desires that they love Him—and their neighbors—and life itself . . . and He wants even the loving to be a growing, developing experience.

Our Father continually calls young men and women to the ministry of the college campus, but the Church often fails to understand the importance of the call. And few men and women are interested in making the necessary sacrifices.

As you can see, I am very pleased about your young minister's becoming a campus minister. I have been writing to you concerning the habits of a full life, for your use in advising the young minister. His entry onto a university campus will require that he become a serious student, himself. Encourage him to study! Our Father has given humans an astounding ability to reason, to deduce, and to analyze. Their ability is much like ours! Their senses are lacking in comparison to ours, but their minds are quite adequate. Pity how little they use them! Many tears are shed in heaven as we helplessly see humans replace their reasoning powers with bigotry and prejudice: the workings of small minds. The enemy has developed a special school to teach his workers how to implant closed mental attitudes in humans.

An inquiring mind is always a thrill to behold. The human philosopher, Peter Abelard, said that the truth humans discern by faith is the same as the truth they discern by reason. His point was that truth is truth, and that it always is of God. God gave humans both religious faith and the power of reason. Abelard perceived that both are important to God . . . that an open and inquiring mind is an essential part of God's plan for humans—as essential as faith.

The most successful method of opening human minds is to establish the habit of regular study. God has been revealing His truths to humans throughout the centuries. The opportunity to learn what our Father has revealed is endless. An active, growing mind is rarely overcome by despair or any other trouble. If the mind is engaged in constantly seeking our Father and His truth, He reveals Himself in glorious ways.

And so, my nephew, as your young minister worships and works, so he must seek God with his whole mental effort—in order to find the full life. The university setting is ideal. It not only affords him a place in which to serve, it requires of him an active mind to minister to the humans around him!

Affectionately,
Uncle Gabriel

XIX

HABITS OF THE FULL LIFE: FELLOWSHIP

Dear Angelique,

Ah, how seldom humans realize the glories which they can experience in their relationships together! Our Father has endowed human creatures with the gift of love so they can know fellowship much like the joy of Heaven. The human spirit has been prepared for friendship with God. It can fly—even on earth!

Quite often, individuals get a chance to experience in their lives, first hand, a glimpse of God. It might be an opportunity to do something really nice for someone in need, and the pleasure of the act is so much more than they expected. It might be in meeting someone who is so filled with God's love that he or she sparkles with a special joy in living. It might be in the stumbling upon some hidden truth that brings new meaning and purpose to life. It might be the experience of falling in love and realizing the truth that such love is a special gift from God.

When these individuals find each other—individuals who have experienced the joy of love—often small groups of them come together to experiment with this divine love. They gather together for a few days at a camp or religious "retreat" and attempt to live on the highest levels of loving fellowships. We could not be more pleased. They live for a while forgetting self and absorbing the cares and needs of those souls around them. Miracles begin to happen. Broken souls and bodies find healing. Our Father is in their midst with a power which very nearly overwhelms them with joy. Their soul-growth during these times is extremely rapid. Those who experience such fellowship are never the same again.

One of the great purposes to which we angels are called (as guardians to humans) is to promote the experience of divine fellowship among them. The problem that we face, however, is that the enemy has a very easy time discouraging it. There are several reasons why some humans never experience this joy of divine fellowship. The reasons involve both the way humans are made . . . their basic nature . . . but also involve the active, diabolic purposes of the enemy as he attempts his destruction.

Human individuality, which is a sacred God-given trust, can be a separating force—at least in its early stages. The enemy can distort this divine gift into selfishness and even bigotry. When he succeeds in the distortion, the humans with whom he succeeds will never know that their individuality is God's plan to create them to be like Himself. This plan is that they be God's children who grow up to inherit His Kingdom.

Heaven, remember, is where each soul has grown to its fullest potential as a separate, distinct creature—loving and respecting every other separate, distinct creature. We want humans to learn to love so that they can experience the heavenly fellowship on earth. In contrast, the enemy uses individuality to cause a soul to turn in on itself and thus see others as worthless. This self-centeredness causes the individual soul to imprison itself in its own separateness.

Humans, like all creatures, are instilled with the desire for self-preservation, a physical requirement for survival. Our Father's plan is for them to learn that the secret for their eternal health is in caring for others. Their lives on the earth-planet give them the opportunity to grow out of *self-preservation* into *self-giving*. The enemy uses the human desire for self-preservation and lures humans to believe that it is their right to satisfy this desire at the expense and exploitation of all other humans. He has little difficulty in suppressing the more important truth: that only in self-giving is there real life.

Humans are given a beautiful ability to trust each other. It is a fragile quality, easily destroyed. A successful tactic of the enemy is the destroying of trust by shrewdly placing distrust in their minds. I am not speaking of the natural absence of trust which one might expect to find between strangers. I am speaking of an active, diabolical distrust, implanted in the human mind, which grips and kills the soul.

God's plan is for humans to learn trust. Trust is the foundation of all good relationships. Trust is the basic ingredient of real faith. When the enemy succeeds in destroying trust, he undercuts the hope for divine fellowship.

The divine plan is that humans learn basic principles of fellowship through their close relationships with family members and friends. But many humans come from broken homes and never know fellowship, even with their human parents. Thus they never treasure the sacred hope of love with their fellow humans, much less with our Father. Therefore, the cultivation of fellowship is a very important priority. It must be one of the daily disciplines of your young minister as he develops the habits of the full life.

Fellowship begins with our Father. All love, all fellowship comes from Him. Here in Heaven, in our prayers, in our devotions, we open our lives to fellowship with Him. Humans are the same. As our Father's love surrounds your young minister's heart, and he opens his life to that love and allows it to enter his heart, then it spreads out to his family and friends. Divine fellowship begins to happen.

One of the privileges of the calling to be a minister is that your young man constantly has the opportunity to encourage fellowship and to experiment with it in his congregation. After all, the ideal Church—the real Church—is the "priesthood of believers," the "fellowship of reconciliation," the redemptive "fellowship," the "communion of saints."

True fellowship is indeed rare—even in the Church! I hope to see your young minister working with his students that they might catch just one glimpse of the warm joy of love. It can transform their group into a force for truth—even in an embittered time of a confused world.

Encourage your young minister to seek divine fellowship for his fellow humans. Keep reminding him that the required ingredient for the divine fellowship is the giving of himself to others, because the very thrust of creation is our Father's eternal giving.

With love,
Uncle Gabriel

XX

JEALOUSY AND THE COMPLETE LOVE OF GOD

Dear Angelique,

Yes, your young minister is dealing with a very human situation! The problem which you describe and which to us seems so trivial, even humorous, can cause a very tragic experience for the persons your young minister is being called upon to counsel. We are delighted that he has found such happiness in his marriage and family life. We predicted, you will remember, that he and his wife would grow into a beautiful life together. His own experience will help him in his marriage counseling.

You tell me that his campus congregation has employed a new choir director, and that she is a lovely and talented young woman. And she has become a close friend with the young baritone whom she is helping with voice lessons. Members of the choir have spoken to the young minister, because they see trouble brewing and feel that he should intervene. Their motivations are mixed between genuine concern and just the "talk" of meddlesome people.

I am sure, as you say, that the two do not yet suspect the potential dangers. The choir director is married. The young baritone is married. The close relationship which is developing between them could become threatening to the choir director's husband and to the young baritone's wife. Some humans cannot believe that a human male and a human female can work closely together, even develop strong ties of friendship with each other, and still remain loyal to their marriage partners. And so, they must deal with the problem of *jealousy*, even though the relationship is a great—and innocent—friendship.

For us in Heaven, jealousy does not exist. In our lives, glory comes by loving more. Jealousy does not exist in Heaven, because our joy is in loving. We have no experience of our love being threatened by those whom we love also loving others. For us, it is a sheer delight to see our fellow angels grow and expand their love to include more and more souls.

Contrary to what many humans think, jealousy is not a form of love. Jealousy is the opposite of love, akin to hate (actually a form of hate), resulting from a malady which we call "heart shrinkage." Jealousy is self-serving—selfish . . . while love is self-giving—selfless.

Jealousy is a force foreign to us, because it is a malady designed and produced by the enemy . . . one of his favorite curses. He has been very successful in introducing jealousy into the human love experience. He has convinced many humans that jealousy is a necessary part of their loyalty to their beloved. We have lost many, many wonderful human families to this deception.

Let me pause to remind you of a basic part of our Father's nature. As we consider the human problem of jealousy, we must point out the contrast between human jealousy and God's complete love. But to understand God's complete love, we must remember that a very real part of His love is His special care for humans in pain—humans with many different forms of need. This special love, if misunderstood, could give other humans a misconception of being left out . . . the possibility of not being loved, of being slighted by God. It could lead to humans being jealous of other humans whom they think might receive more of God's goodness than themselves. It is, indeed, a matter related to the whole of human jealousy!

It is true that God does have His special favorites. My old acquaintance, Screwtape, one of our enemy's officers (I have mentioned him to you before), has said in one of his famous *Screwtape Letters*, collected some years ago by Professor C. S. Lewis:

" . . . some of His (God's) special favourites go through longer and deeper troughs than anyone else."

Screwtape was describing human peaks of inspiration and deep troughs of despair. He was referring to the extremes of human happiness and human suffering. He knows God can use both for human growth.

Our Father's love is complete. His having special favorites represents not that He loves some less. His love for each soul is complete. *There can be no greater love than God's love for each single soul.* But under certain circumstances, He does seem to love some souls more. The Son expressed this idea in his parable of the lost sheep. He said that the shepherd leaves ninety-nine of his hundred sheep untended—in danger—if he needs to go in search of one that is lost. He said there is more rejoicing in Heaven over his finding the one that was lost, than over the ninety-nine that were not lost.

God loves each of the "ninety-nine" completely. But He does seem to have a very special care—a special love, a favoritism—for the lost, for the needy. It is like the love that the Psalmist expressed in the Bible's *Twenty-third Psalm.* He said that his "cup overflows," because of God's care for him. God fills every soul's cup, but some He seems to overfill.

God loves each soul completely. God surrounds each soul with His love. But He actually enters and becomes one with some souls. The Son described the hungry, the thirsty, the stranger, the naked, the sick, and the imprisoned . . . and said that as we care for them, we care for him. He has become one with the needy. God's special favorites are those in need. That God has special favorites simply means that the needy—those who for whatever reason need God's love more—receive the additional love that they require to be whole, to be complete.

When our Father created humans, He made them free, yet incomplete. His purpose was that they might grow. *Freedom and incompleteness are the stuff out of which come children of God!* When humans experience the magnificence of God's love, they cease to want to be the *only* favorite. They, like we, become dedicated to the inclusiveness of God's love—His great love for all souls. It is then that they have begun their real growth toward fellowship with God (which is the soul's potential for completeness).

We speak of God's favorites—His love for the needy—to show the magnificence of His love and how different it is from the littleness of human jealousy and lack of love. Yet herein is the answer to your minister's problem with the choir director and the baritone. The answer is not in telling them to love less, but in helping them to find the highest levels of love in both their friendships and in their marriages. As they find these high levels of love, they find God . . . they find the magnificence of His love.

Tell your young minister to keep reminding them of the great joy they have and will continue to have because of the gifts of spouse and family.

They can keep the experience of friendship alive in many creative ways. They have the resources to maintain strong friendships as well as their deep marriage love. The four all have been blessed in their marriages with the rich experience of God's love because of their marriages. They know love of the highest form: the special gift of divine love which God gives to couples in love.

Yet strange as it may seem, they are particularly susceptible to the dangers of other's jealousy. They have learned to love openly. They have an innocence which makes them unaware of jealousy. Having experienced God's complete love, they have a bit of Heaven on earth. They have joy . . . and humans who have not experienced the divine fellowship—the complete love of God—do not understand the joy.

Our Father's Kingdom is not yet on earth. His earth is a place where humans have the opportunity to learn of and experience His complete love. When His Kingdom comes on Earth as it is in Heaven, there will be no jealousy. All humans will love each other. All parents will love all children. All children will love all parents. As there will be no hatred, there will be no death. All men will love all women. All women will love all men. Temptation will have passed away—not because human sexuality is bad, but because it is good. It is very good.

Indeed, human sexuality is one of the most beautiful and glorious aspects of our Father's creation of humans. Through their sexuality, humans learn to love God. The most glorious experience of romantic love, known by human male and female in the full marriage commitment, is a marvelous glimpse of the love known by souls in Heaven.

Help your young minister to advise the two couples. Remind him that our Father has blessed humans with the ability to experience great joy in close, loving friendships . . . and in the home with family . . . and in a sacred love for their mates. God has given a part of Himself to humans in friendships and in their family love and especially in their marriage love.

With deep affection,
Uncle Gabriel

XXI

HABITS OF THE FULL LIFE: RECREATION

Dear Angelique,

We have been discussing the habits of the full life, and I am glad that you have asked about recreation and fun and what part they should play in the life of a human who lives for our Father. We must remember that we angels are creatures and not the Creator—a fact we sometimes forget. We cannot fully know God. Yet we do know that He has a magnificent sense of humor, a sense of fun, which He has shared with us and with humans (indeed, all real humor is of God).

There is great work to do. Many souls live in the misery of ignorance, and our Father is calling us and many humans like your young minister to tell of the "glad tidings of great joy." Often we who are committed to the ways of our Father become engulfed in the seriousness of our task and forget the inherent meaning of life: that it is a fullness, a great joy! We must encourage humans to practice the presence of God in all of their lives: their worship, their work, and their leisure. No human has a full life, without fun. I have first-wing knowledge that our Father is delighted with human fun.

Of course, all human activities can be invaded by the enemy. If he can redirect their fun to some selfish motivation of exorbitant monetary gain . . . or change healthy competition into a force that divides humans into snobbish segments . . . or, through humans already won to himself, exploit the beauty of youth to destroy the beauty and the youth . . . then it is indeed the enemy's field day!

However, our Father gives humans many creative ways to have fun . . . ways that are truly re-creative. We can assume certain guidelines for fun which may help you in advising your young minister.

First, the fun must not be for one human at another human's expense. It must be mutually beneficial to all. Much human humor is directed toward laughing at the supposed inferiority of another human or group of humans. The enemy is always present in such humor. It is destructive of soul.

Another guideline to remember is that good fun should help take humans outside of themselves. We of the angelic realm have learned the bitter lesson of the enemy: that obsession with self is the most destructive of all forces. It causes the soul to be trapped inside itself. The imprisonment of the soul is Satan's strategic war aim. He keeps the prison! God's plan is that the soul be free. In human history, the major battles for righteousness have encouraged humans to "lose" themselves . . . get beyond selfishness . . . for God's sake. But it is in times of everyday fun that humans begin to practice the habit of losing themselves in the joy of life and in concern for others. Their games teach them the importance of teamwork . . . the phenomenon of souls losing themselves for each other.

Humans are greatly concerned with competition, and human games give them a wonderful opportunity to explore the good and evil of competition. I must remind you that we have some difficulty understanding human competition, for our motivation for good comes from our total awareness of the goodness of God. But human awareness of God's goodness is much more protected . . . it sometimes is even hidden from their sight. It is true that through various forms of competition, they are motivated to do their best work. We often would like to break through their blindness and show them pure beauty. But we must remember our Father's plan is for them to choose freely. In this sense, their blindness is their blessing, and with their blindness they work harder in their world when they fear that another human might do their job better than they. The harder work shows the qualities of good competition.

In their recreation, humans divide into teams, and the teams oppose each other. The competition which is thus generated is good insofar as it raises the spirit of fun and friendliness. However, I must warn that competition can be very dangerous. It has a tendency to raise human emotions to a very high intensity. After all, competition is a form of battle. It sets human against human. Battles create enemies. God's plan is that humanity should take the form a relationship of brothers, sisters, and friends. Competition begins as friendly games, but given human emotions, it can get out of control. As soon as competition reaches a point of enmity, or snobbery (the weakness which allows some humans to think that they are better children of the Father than others), then it becomes the enemy's day.

Human games can teach the thrill of unity through participation in a common cause. Humans separate themselves so easily into warring factions. They divide over their place or nation of birth, over their racial color, over their material wealth, and even over their views of our Father. They seem to find it important to make these divisions, and then they build walls between the divisions.

One might think that their games, where they divide into opposing teams, simply would create more bad divisions. But actually, their games have had the effect of teaching them unity, not diversity. So long as they remember that defeating their opponent is not the primary purpose of their games, and that a reasonable purpose is just fun, the Spirit of our Father with His joy invades their games. They discover that all are working and playing together as brothers, sisters, and friends—even the members of opposing teams.

Games generally divide humans into winners and losers. On the surface, such division would appear to be a bad thing. In Heaven, we think of "winning" as the victory of spirit which accompanies communion with our Father. "Losing," to us, represents a soul's choice of self: Satan's way over God's way.

For humans, winning and losing may have little meaning—the purely innocent matter of the result of their games. However, humans may learn great lessons in their winning and losing. In winning, humans can experience a sense of accomplishment. They hopefully learn humility and respect for their fellow humans. In losing, humans have the opportunity to learn the marvelous lesson of sportsmanship: that today's loss is temporary and that the goals of life remain ever available.

I think of the player who falls face down in the mud. In sports, that player is taught to get up and go on . . . to never "give up." It is the lesson that *no human is ever beyond the reach of our Father and His healing spirit*; and that the opponent on the game field really is the brother, sister, and friend. Granted, in simple human games, the lessons are only symbolic—yet they are great lessons of truth.

I heard an interesting story from your earth-planet recently. It seems that young children were being taught the game of "soccer," and the lessons of sportsmanship were being promoted as "life lessons." In a game, one very talented girl was out front with a clear shot at the goal, when from the side she saw an opposing player fall hurt. Instead of going for the goal, the girl turned abruptly aside and went to help the hurt player. The coach reprimanded her severely, telling her,

"Never ever let me catch you doing that again! Winning isn't just everything . . . *It is the only thing!*"

Nonsense! Angelique, I cannot tell you how terrible such an idea is—or how completely it contradicts the concept of sportsmanship—or, therefore, how destructive it is of the whole purpose of sports!

Many benefits come to humans in their fun: They are freed from their imprisoned feelings of defeat and bitterness (which the enemy cleverly places in their hearts). They develop more healthy bodies and minds (not unimportant in human life). They become more aware of beauty as their minds relax through play; and then they can participate with our Father in the creating of beauty . . . through art and music and dance. As they play together and enjoy life more, they learn more reverence for life. Their play becomes an awareness of God!

My nephew, the very subject of fun and the full life fills my soul with joy. As I write of it, I find laughter in Heaven. Human fun, too, brings laughter. We must remember that laughter is one of the great healing and cleansing gifts of our Father, which He has so graciously given to us and to humans. In times of great tragedy, there are two great healing powers. Ministers of God know the healing power of the message of Christ's self-sacrificing love and victory over death. Many do not realize the marvelous healing power of laughter. I have seen them in great pain—on their death beds—alone and seemingly forsaken; and God's spirit of love and joy has risen within them to the sound of great laughter, and their souls are cleansed and healed and made pure. If there is a force which always defeats the enemy, it is the force of joyous laughter. There is no humor in Hell.

In His fun,
Uncle Gabriel

XXII

HABITS OF A FULL LIFE:
CREATIVITY IN HUMANS

Dear Angelique,

In our discussion of the habits of the full life, we should not omit the fact that humans, like ourselves, must regularly exercise a special gift from our Father: the gift of His creative power. It is the gift of a part of His own Being. When our Father created the first humans, He put a divine spark into them. He actually shared His essence with humans as He had shared it with angels. His nature is eternal Love, and from that nature, constant and continuing newness is born—is created. What a magnificent gift He has given! Humans, like us, on a small scale participate in divine creativity! The creation of the human soul was a result of God's nature: to love.

But human fears and anxieties can cover and surround the spark and very nearly extinguish it. The enemy has trained his troops to become agile in the de-art of depressing humans to the point of the stagnation of this divine creativity. We must not allow it! Our guardians, like yourself, must be encouraging humans to exercise their special gift, each earth-day of their lives.

The creative impulse in humans can break through in many ways. Some humans express their creativity best in their work. In a wide variety of vocations, they draw on a power beyond the mere mechanical, beyond habit. There are teachers and lawyers and doctors and business persons who use their imaginations and energies creatively to cross new thresholds of thought and service.

Other humans exercise their talents through their many interests called hobbies. Thus, a mathematician who works with numbers all day may go home and paint beautiful landscapes. Or an accountant, in her spare time, may become interested in collecting rare works of art and even leave the world of numbers for the world of art. A bricklayer may compose fine music. Or a young student may be in a church choir and sing beautiful cantatas. Oh, the wonders of divine creativity in humans!

My nephew, let me give you some advice on recognizing the creative impulse in humans so that you may encourage it. Among humans, oratory or speaking in public, is a great art. It requires ability, training, and much hard work. But above all, oratory is a creative process . . . an art mastered by very few. Your young minister regularly speaks in public. He is one who has determined to master the art. His speeches and sermons are usually quite commendable. Much of his success is the result of years of training. Much is hard study and thorough preparation. But every once in a while, during a speech, our Father finds an opening in your young minister's life and thoughts . . . an opening born of the deep human desire for God . . . and God and your young minister for a moment become one. A new creation takes place! The experience is magnificent! Your young minister knows what is happening: that what he is saying is of an experience beyond himself. It is a moment of inspiration. Because of that moment of openness, God speaks through him. Because of that oneness with God, words become relatively unimportant.

His listeners understand, because God's Spirit is there, and the communication is of the Spirit. Life, death, and eternity are all bound up in that moment. His listeners say that he reaches great eloquence. Some felt a new joy in the air about them. The listeners may not know what is happening, but it is God at work in your young minister . . . creating, changing, building, making new, and expressing His great truth. God expresses that truth in humans who invest the time and energy to train themselves for a vocation, who are determined to achieve excellence in it, and who are willing to open themselves to our Father. One such moment makes the many years of preparation worthwhile. It is a rare experience for humans. The human mind and body are not accustomed to maintaining such excitement so familiar to us in Heaven.

Creativity takes place in many ways. The writer creates new thoughts or a new arrangement of old thoughts. The craftsman molds new objects of beauty or usefulness. The artist paints a new picture or composes new music. The musician performs and the gardener helps plants and flowers to grow. The laborer builds a bridge and the artisan creates a violin. But whether it is a gardener helping a rose bush to blossom into the glorious color of a mountain sunset, or a minister becoming a channel for our Father's Word, the experience of creativity is there—a magnificent gift of the divine from our Father.

Encourage your young minister to participate in the many creative interests which are naturally his, in his work and in his hobbies. The enemy knows only destructiveness. Creativity throws him into a maze of confusion. Can you imagine an architect designing a great cathedral in Hell . . . or Michelangelo (I do like that name!) painting the ceiling of the Sistine Chapel under the *ex*spiration of Satan?

Love,
Uncle Gabe

XXIII

FEAR OF DEATH

Dear Angelique,

Your recent letter, describing your young minister's attitude during his conducting of the funeral service for a member of his church, causes me to be happy about your guardianship. Your young minister's understanding of God's plan to give humans the inheritance of His Kingdom—to give mortals eternal life—is maturing nicely. But his attitude upset some of the members of the congregation. He needs help in dealing with them. He, unlike them, has grown in faith to see that the death of the human body promises the beginning of an even greater life with God. He also understands that humans need not worry about our care for them after they leave their earthly existence. He knows that we will never allow permanent harm to come to them. God's love is eternal!

However, what your young minister does not seem to remember is that most humans are terrified when confronted with that time of change. They call it "death" (a term we use in connection with the destruction of the soul, as when creatures allow themselves to become possessions of the enemy . . . and even that destruction we believe not to be final). Of course, it is true that the earthly body dies. The earthly body is a temporary home, a stage of life. The soul goes on to a better home. Yet, when facing death, humans experience a terror so intense that most of them fear the sound of the word and will not allow themselves even to think of it.

It is very difficult for humans to be separated from the ones they love, even for a short while. Remember that they cannot see the fullness of eternity. Our Father's plan for them limits their vision to their own day, with a few memories, and very little understanding of their future. Thus, eternity is a great mystery to them. God has given them His promises, but they receive these promises only through their faith and their hope. Their faith is a trust in our Father's love. Their hope is a trust that this faith is their true contract with what is real and good. Faith and hope are divine gifts.

You see, our Father's plan for humans is to give it all to them—even the gift of Himself. But such a plan holds great danger for the human soul. Humans must be free. If humans knew of God's gift . . . if they had knowledge of eternity through any other than the beautiful glimpses . . . the awe produced would be the equivalent of slavery. For humans to see the full greatness of God would be to overwhelm them with truth so sure that they could not turn away from it. They would have no choices. They would have no freedom. The human soul must be free, free to soar. And God wants humans to soar. Choices must be made without sure knowledge of the result. Choices must be made on faith alone. Life with God comes by faith, and faith must have freedom.

Our Father does not want humans to be afraid of death. But He cannot show them the fullness of eternity . . . not yet. Temporary fear of death is better than permanent slavery. Therefore, even though fear can be very destructive, and death, a frightening mystery for humans, these experiences are necessary. They are parts of God's plan to withhold sure knowledge of eternity from humans for their own good. The mortal soul is prepared for sure knowledge of eternity only after it has wrestled with its selfishness and given up that selfishness. Then the soul must choose to face the fear of the unknown. When it is ready to face the fear of the unknown, it will find that the unknown is known by God and need not be feared. Few humans in your young minister's realm are ready for that discovery. They still want to hold on to their self-centeredness, and they have a great fear of the mysteries of death.

And so when your young minister last week criticized the rituals and methods by which humans dispose of their used-up bodies, he struck a very tender nerve among his people. These rituals are their ways of covering their self-centeredness, hiding their fear, and refusing to face the pain of grief. (We are amazed at their attempts to preserve dead bodies against a useful return to natural elements—and at their pagan ceremonies surrounding the attempts!) I am afraid that some of the members of your young minister's church do not understand his joy and thanksgiving at the time of death. They think that he is being irreverent, or even that he is mocking their grief.

Grief is a very real part of human existence. Humans develop very close relationships with each other. Their friends and loved ones are an actual part of their own understanding of themselves. When a love relationship breaks up, or (as in your young minister's present situation) one of his flock dies and leaves loved ones to grieve the loss, the humans who are left alone on the earth-planet experience their deepest pain: the sense of aloneness. They are not alone, of course, but they feel alone, and the pain overwhelms them. That pain is in fact grief.

Your young minister is growing in faith to sense that the love of God completely surrounds humans at all times, but especially surrounds them when they are in pain. Our purpose as guardians is to help humans know God's presence. Their pain is real. They need to know that God's presence is the greater reality. Your young minister is learning to understand, and it gives him joy. He also sees glimpses of the great eternity for those who have died.

You must help him interpret for his church members his sense of joy at this passing of a friend into a new and glorious life. Most of his church members have never experienced any such joy and thus have no basis for understanding it. Help him remember that humans have great difficulty in believing that the new and glorious life exists. Help him to remind his church members that with God all things are possible. They need not worry about life after death. They will be in good hands. God has great plans for every human soul.

Eternally,
Uncle Gabe

XXIV

GENESIS ONE IN THE 21st CENTURY

Dear Angelique,

For some time I have been planning to talk to you about Creation. Being a young angel, you have no way of knowing; and earth-people are becoming so knowledgeable about their beginnings, that they realize that the stories in their Bible are inaccurate, if read literally. As a matter of fact, the stories can be misleading with regard to our Father's purpose for humans.

Their Bible has two creation stories. The first one, related in the first chapter of Genesis, is a beautiful hymn celebrating our Father's creativity in six stages, followed by a seventh stage, the time of His resting and hallowing the creation. The second story, which is actually the older of the two in its written form, tells of the Garden of Eden and the two humans put in the Garden by God. The wisdom of those ancient stories as their writers recognized God's great work, represents that God was beginning to show Himself clearly to humans. That they understood earth to be flat and heaven to be a dome does not detract from their awareness of beauty and truth as God revealed beauty and truth to them.

The writers did not know the whole truth. Only God knows the whole truth. But if those writers had been living now in the 21st earth-century after Christ, with the knowledge that their philosophers and scientists and theologians have gathered in the centuries since the Bible writing, and with the abundance of revelations which God has given in those centuries, they would have written differently. One of our young guardians, Orthodoxus, sent me a copy of such a 21st Century writing. It has merit . . . though later writers will learn more, grow in their understanding, and, hopefully, change their writings. So, I pass it on to you:

GENESIS ONE in the TWENTY-FIRST CENTURY

"In the beginning God created the heavens and the earth. The creation was without form and void, and darkness was upon the face of the void; and the Spirit of God was moving over the face of space.

And God said, 'Let there be light,' and there was a burst of light. And the light dispelled the darkness. And God saw that the light was good. And there was evening and there was morning, one divine day.

And God said, 'Let there be stars in space—a universe.' And God rolled up great masses of light and power, and threw them out into space, filling the void with the stars. He gathered the stars into galaxies . . . over a hundred billion stars in each galaxy. And the galaxies were given names, one the Milky Way . . . another, its twin, Andromeda. And God separated the galaxies in distances so vast that light, traveling at the speed of over six hundred million miles per hour, took two million years to reach from one galaxy to another.

And one of the stars God called the Sun. And God placed the Sun in the Milky Way. And it was so. And there was evening and there was morning, a second divine day.

And God said, 'Let there be planets.' And gaseous spheres of fire from the Sun began to circle around the Sun to establish the seasons and the years. And one of the planets God called Earth. And from the Earth, God slung the Moon to circle the Earth and be a lesser light to rule the Earth's night. And God cooled the Earth for over a billion years, gradually forming the seas and the dry land, the great mountains and the rivers that flowed to the seas. He formed the glaciers of ice, and the air, and the clouds which filled the sky and brought the rain. And the rains fell upon the Earth. And God set the Earth turning, that the light from the Sun might cause Night and Day, cool and heat, shade and light. And God saw that it was good. And there was evening and there was morning, a third divine day.

And God said, 'Let there be living things,' and the miracle of life began. God took a small piece of lifeless matter, giving it part of His own life, and made a one-celled plant and put it in the sea. And from that one-celled plant in the sea God began forming all of the different varieties of life, each with the power to develop and to change and to become something better, molded by God's plan. So God created the sea plants, forests of living plants under the waters of the Earth. And God saw that life was good. And there was evening and there was morning, a fourth divine day.

And God said, 'Let there be animals in the seas, and from the living sea plants God made creatures that lived in shells . . . and fishes that moved through the waters. And God said, 'Let the sea plants spread to the dry land. 'Let the earth put forth vegetation, plants yielding seed, and fruit trees bearing fruit in which is their seed.' And the mountains and valleys became green with ferns and grasses and forests of trees. And God saw that it was good. And there was evening and there was morning, a fifth divine day.

And God said, 'Let animals come out onto the land, and breathe, and multiply, and fly.' So God made the beasts of the earth and the tiny insects and the great reptiles. He made the birds and the cattle and the little creeping things. And God saw that it was good.

Then God said, 'Let us make humans in our image, after our likeness; and let them have dominion over the fish of the sea, and over the birds of the air, and over the cattle, and over all the earth, and over every creeping thing that creeps upon the earth.' From a piece of His own soul God made the human soul, male and female He created them, crowning over three billion years of life . . . ever changing, ever growing, ever developing life: humans, the greatest of all His creation miracles—alive, individual, intelligent, and free—to inherit His Kingdom. And God blessed them. And God saw everything that He had made, and behold, it was very good. And there was evening and there was morning, a sixth divine day.

And on the seventh divine day, God rested. He blessed and hallowed the seventh day and established it as a day of rest and worship. And, thus, His creation was begun. There was much more to do, to create. And so, God's great hand continues to invent, to change, to build, and to work, that His Kingdom will come on Earth as it is in His Heaven. Amen."

* * *

Angelique, this document is by a human writer who has much to learn about God's greatness—beyond his wildest dreams! We, of course, are delighted when humans discover new truths. That is God's plan for their growth and their freedom. Our angelic task is to help them in every possible way. I have more to write to you about the Garden of Eden, but that must wait. St. Peter seems to be having some difficulty and needs me at the Gate. I will write again, soon.

Love,
Uncle Gabe

XXV

THE GARDEN OF EDEN REVISITED

Dear Angelique,

I apologize for stopping rather abruptly in my last letter. An earth person was creating quite a scene, demanding heavenly entry. It seems that the human had made some sort of deal with a clergyman in one of our earth-churches. He had been told that he would be assured entry, if he gave a large financial contribution toward the construction of a prayer chapel in this clergyman's church. We had to explain to him that he needed to learn how to use that prayer chapel. More to the point, we explored with him his mind and heart in regard to his attitudes about his fellow humans. He has much to learn, but his soul is not forgotten. He will be back . . . oh, I must remember to talk to Benedictus, our guardian in charge of human church officials, about that clergyman.

I wanted to write to you about the Garden of Eden. The story, as told in the Bible, gives us great cause for concern. It was a long time between the events in the lives of those early humans and the writing, and some of the facts were lost. The story is a mixture of historic events, religious belief, and metaphor or parable: a story symbolizing important truths. Adam and Eve, whom God put in the garden, representing the earliest humans, are described as living in a kind of paradise—a place where they have plenty to eat, no worries or troubles, and living in innocence. Their only responsibility in the garden was "to till it and keep it." The writers of the story apparently thought that our Father did not intend for humans to have intelligence; that He did not want them to think; that He did not want them to discover the difference between good and evil; that He did not want them to have freedom; and that He did not want them to have responsibility beyond the tilling and the keeping of the garden. The story suggests that our Father forbade humans to eat the fruit of the Tree of the Knowledge of Good and Evil.

It is important for you to understand that God did want them to eat this fruit . . . just not yet! (They were not mature enough to accept the responsibility.) The Tree of the Knowledge of Good and Evil did not bear the forbidden fruit. There was forbidden fruit. The Tree of Hate (not included in the Bible story) bore the forbidden fruit . . . more about the Tree of Hate later. The fruit of the Knowledge of Good and Evil was, in fact, to be a gift from God. It was to be the gift which separated humans from lower animals. Through this fruit, our Father intended to bestow upon humans His own Spirit. He intended to blow into them the breath of His Spirit, the breath of divine life.

The important trees in the Garden of Eden were five:

1) The Tree of Life
2) The Tree of Survival
3) The Tree of the Knowledge of Good and Evil
4) The Tree of Hate
5) The Tree of Love

The Bible story suggests that there were many trees in the garden, but the trees of Survival, Hate, and Love are not mentioned by name.

God has spent a very long time developing His human creatures on the earth-planet. Remember His ultimate purpose: He is creating souls for fellowship . . . for the loving relationship that completes joy, that ends loneliness, that conquers evil and selfishness, that makes suffering a privilege and thus ends suffering, and that is the death of death for it is eternal life. The fellowship is, indeed, the gift of Heaven, God's ultimate purpose in creation!

To achieve this fellowship, our Father had to create souls that He could set free. It was a project which took over three billion earth-years. He started with the miracle of life. From no-life, He made life. We angles do not understand how He achieved the miracle. We know that he used a part of Himself. All of life has the divine source. Only God can create life. He put the first tree, the Tree of Life, in Eden.

The "Tree if Life" on the earth-planet began as a one-celled plant in the earth's sea. But simple life was only the beginning. The Tree of Life holds another of God's miracles. This second miracle is a process which humans have trouble believing, because they think that somehow it belittles them. They think that "evolution" means that they are descended from lesser creatures, like monkeys. (They would rather believe that they are made from dust!) In a sense, it is true that we all are *descended* from lesser creatures. But the greater truth is an *ascending*. Each generation of life for over three billion earth-years has been given newer and higher levels of divine purpose and divine help. God has combined newer and greater amounts of freedom and intelligence with new types and complexities of life. The creative process has been constant. The fruit of the Tree of Life holds the miracle for this creative process. Humans call it *evolution*.

The second tree in the garden, the Tree of Survival, also has an important place in Eden. On the earth-planet, in the world of nature, survival is tough, but a necessity for life. In order for an earth-animal to live in a sometimes hostile, always competitive environment, that creature must learn to care for itself, to survive. And caring for self is a basically selfish but natural act. The earth-animal must get food; it must find and defend its shelter or territory; it must defend itself against its enemies and the forces of nature which attempt to destroy it. It must for a time elude death. And if its species is to survive, it must find a mate and produce offspring. These survival requirements are all basically selfish but at this point in the development of life, not in any way sinful. Survival is a natural need.

This tradition of natural selfishness is passed on to humans. Every human is born with selfish instincts—natural needs which manifest themselves in human life as hunger, pride, jealousy, desire for sex, obsession with possessions, and many other forms of natural selfishness. Lower animals satisfy these selfish needs by eating the fruit of the Tree of Survival. Humans, too, must eat this fruit in the early stages of their development, and the eating of it is not evil. In this fruit is the nourishment for a kind of innocence and a kind of goodness: innocence because this fruit is created for creatures who are not responsible for moral decisions; goodness because all creatures of God share in the goodness of God . . . His world is created good. However, *original sin* comes from the fruit of this Tree of Survival, because selfishness is the source of sin.

Remember, selfishness is not sin, yet. The state of sin is the state of being separated from God. *To sin* is to do those things, think those thoughts, and have those attitudes which separate one from God. Natural selfishness is merely the fulfillment of the natural need for survival. It cannot become sin until the creature eats the fruit of the third tree, the Tree of the Knowledge of Good and Evil which, as we said, God planned for them to eat. It was God's plan that when humans began to stand on their own and make decisions, the fruit of the Tree of the Knowledge of Good and Evil would be made available to them. With the eating of this fruit comes an awareness of the responsibility for one's individual life, for the lives of other individuals, and for society as a whole. It is a frightening gift of God, that humans are invited to be responsible souls. Sadly enough, some humans in their earthly existence never learn to stand on their own and make decisions. And so, they never eat this fruit and never learn the great benefits of it—they are never human in the fullest sense.

In Eden, the serpent, representing Satan, the enemy of God, was the first to offer humans this fruit of the third tree, the Tree of the Knowledge of Good and Evil, as the Bible story says. Satan did not gain or lose by humans eating fruit of the second tree, the Survival fruit, and had no intention of waiting for God's plan to unfold. Satan needed for humans to know the difference between right and wrong in order to be able to do his work with them.

After eating the Knowledge of Good and Evil fruit, humans knew right from wrong and became responsible for their decisions. If Satan could cause humans to let selfishness dominate these decisions after they had eaten this fruit, then he could have them in his power. You see, *right is that which is creative and useful for individuals and society in leading them toward a loving fellowship. Wrong is that which is destructive of that loving fellowship.* Thus selfishness, which is destructive of fellowship, ceases to be just the fulfillment of natural need and becomes wrong after the eating of the fruit of the Tree of the Knowledge of Good and Evil. It therefore becomes sin. Selfishness separates souls from each other and from God. And it leaves them open to the power of Satan.

Our Father too, wanted humans to eat this fruit, as we have said. Only when humans eat of the Knowledge of Good and Evil fruit, can they grow to the likeness of God, which is God's plan. After gaining the Knowledge of Good and Evil, humans become responsible for choosing between the demonic fruit of the fourth tree, the Tree of Hate, and the divine fruit of the fifth tree, the Tree of Love.

The Tree of Hate bore fruits of greed, pride, prejudice, ugliness, and ignorance. The Tree of Love bore fruits of generosity, humility, compassion, beauty, and truth. As humans all through earth's history choose the fruit of Love, their need for the fruit of Survival lessens; they turn away from the Tree of Hate. They discover the sustaining power of God in the Tree of Love.

The marvelous third tree, the Tree of the Knowledge of Good and Evil, had many fruits: the fruits of individuality and intelligence and freedom, the fruits of soul and mind and heart. It was not the tree that bore the forbidden fruit. The Tree of Hate bore the forbidden fruit—the most serious sin and separation from God. Hate is the final result of sin. Hate is a basic desire for destruction rather than creation, wrong rather than right. But remember: this fruit of the third tree, the Tree of the Knowledge of Good and Evil included the freedom fruit. And freedom allowed humans to eat even the forbidden fruit of Hate!

The enemy was present—the serpent—and his purpose was to lure humans to the forbidden fruit. First, he offered the Knowledge of Good and Evil fruit. Then, he offered the forbidden fruit of Hate which, when eaten, kills love, turns humans from God, and places them under Satan's evil power.

Always, our Father has been leading human creatures from the Knowledge of Good and Evil fruit to the fruit of the last tree, the great tree—the Tree of Love. When they begin to eat this fruit, they begin to be like God, and are prepared for that fellowship about which we have been talking: a loving relationship with God and with each other . . . the ultimate purpose for which they were created.

Angelique, the Tree of Life represents two of God's miracles: the miracle of life from no life and the miracle of progress in life from simple to magnificent. The Tree of Survival represents that life in its early stages requires nurture and has natural needs which are selfish but not evil. The Tree of the Knowledge of Good and Evil represents God's gift of freedom and the responsibility which comes with that freedom. The Tree of Hate is Satan's tree and was in the Garden along with the serpent. It represents freedom's potential power for destruction. And the Tree of Love is God's special tree. It is His hope for His creation.

I hope that these words help to clarify what the Garden of Eden represents. Humans are God's creation. Each one is His special child. He loves them and will always love them. The freedom which He has given them, the real freedom to choose, is filled with dangers but is the breath of His Spirit. Freedom is the road through His love to their inheritance of His Kingdom.

Affectionately,
Uncle Gabe

XXVI

THE GARDEN OF EDEN: PUNISHMENT

Dear Angelique,

You have asked about God's "curse" of the serpent, the woman, and the man in the Garden of Eden. The answer to your question centers around three of the garden's trees: the Knowledge of Good and Evil, Hate, and Love. In the story, as we explained in our last letter, the fruit of Hate was the forbidden fruit. Satan, the enemy, in the form of the serpent, lured Adam and Eve to his Tree of Hate, and they ate.

Already Satan had successfully convinced them to eat the fruit of the Knowledge of Good and Evil—fruit God was not yet ready for them to eat. After Adam and Eve ate the Knowledge of Good and Evil fruit, they had freedom—freedom to make choices. And they, influenced by Satan, chose to eat the forbidden fruit of Hate. The Biblical account suggests that for their disobedience, God punished the serpent, the woman, and the man with severe punishment—punishment that would be passed on for generations to come.

I think that the word "curse" is misleading, suggesting a vengeful act by God. *God has no malice.* But the results of eating this fruit were devastating. Hate is the end result of uncontrolled selfishness. As the Bible account suggests, when they ate the forbidden fruit, Adam and Eve were immediately aware of their nakedness—their sexuality. Nakedness is not evil. The human body is beautiful, and it is good. God made humans naked in Eden, and they still are born naked. But nakedness and sexuality are dangerous. They leave the individual human vulnerable to abuse. And nakedness and sexuality are exploitable, because male and female humans have been given a strong attraction to each other. The Eden story expresses both the goodness and the danger.

After eating the fruit of hate, the innocent relationship between Adam and Eve changed to become the possibility of a desire to possess each other. It really became a contradiction: to own the object of one's love. Lust is the desire to possess and theirs could now become a lust relationship. Instead of loving, which means the giving of self, their disobedience opened the opportunity for lusting, which means the getting of something for self. The sin of lust left them thoroughly confused—possession being a very different relationship from the innocent companionship of equals known to them previously.

The possibility of the sin of lust caused them to be ashamed of their nakedness, and they wanted to hide from God. But it was not only their shame which caused Adam and Eve to hide from God. It was also their guilt for disobeying. When God asked where they were and why they were hiding, He already knew that they were hiding because of their shame and their guilt.

God told the serpent,

"You have given up your rights to the Garden of Eden, because you have committed a great sin."

It was the sin of treason. To plot against God by luring humans to the Tree of Hate and away from the Tree of Love, was an act of treason which established that the serpent was an enemy of God and a creature which could not be trusted. The serpent had chosen the way of untrustworthiness. The serpent was banished from Eden and became the symbol of the enemy of humans as well as the enemy of God.

God told the woman,

"Your disobedience was evil, because I had planned good for you, and your disobedience took you away from My goodness. You have given up your rights to the Garden, and now you must find goodness for yourself in a harsh world. You are free. My love for you will never cease. I will surround you with my care in ways you will not know. I will give to you all that you need to find your way back to me, but your goodness is no longer certain. You must choose goodness in order to return to me."

God told the man,

"Your disobedience also was evil, because I had planned good for you, too. You have given up your rights to the Garden, and now you must work long and hard, and you must search for joy, if you wish to have joy. I set you free as free you were meant to be. Like the woman, you must choose goodness in order to return to me."

God continued,

"You, Adam and Eve, both are my beloved children. But you have chosen to take your inheritance of freedom and go to a far country—that is, far from My ways—after choosing to eat the fruit of selfishness and hate. You have intelligence, and you have the ability to love or to hate. You still have hope. Your souls still are of Me. I made your souls from pieces of My own soul. I will continue to surround you with My love. My love will never cease. My mercies will never come to an end. But much of the time you will not recognize My love or My mercies. You and each of your descendants may accept or reject these gifts."

Then God said,

"Grow toward the Tree of Love . . . turn away from the Tree of Hate and its selfishness . . . and I will give you My Kingdom."

Angelique, remember that God never gives anything but good. The evil which resulted from disobedience in Eden was not God's "curse." Evil is the result of the misuse of the marvelous gifts of God.

Love,
Uncle Gabe

XXVII

THE GARDEN OF EDEN: MAN AND WOMAN

Dear Angelique,

So your young minister is in trouble again! You should have expected the trouble when you supported his inviting a woman to conduct worship and to preach in his church while he was away. Yes, of course God calls women to preach, but many humans feel threatened by the idea of the equality of the sexes.

One of the most serious problems which humans face and must overcome is bigotry. Bigotry takes many forms. Whenever a human sees oneself as better than another human, and believes that this superiority is established by God, that mistaken understanding is bigotry. Each human soul is created by God, and therefore all human souls are equal in His eyes. Differences of race, sex, nation, religion, age, position, or any other uniqueness, do not reflect or represent an inequality of human souls.

The Garden of Eden story has been used for centuries by some humans to establish their superiority over others. Men especially have used it to claim superiority over women. Angelique, our Father did not in the Garden of Eden create the male human superior to the female human.

In the early version of the story, God first created a human creature in His own image. The creature was neither male nor female, but, like God, had all of the qualities of both. The creature was a complete soul, but was alone. The animals which God made did not satisfy the human creature's loneliness. The human creature needed a companion—not a helper, nor a servant—but a companion, an equal partner. And so God divided the human creature into two. Contrary to a traditional belief, God did not take a rib from a man and make a woman. Woman was not made from a small piece of a man. God took a side from the human creature, and that one side was made woman . . . the other side was made man. (There have been errors in many of the translations of the Hebrew Scriptures.) Like a complete picture puzzle with only two pieces, God made the human creature male and female. Each half was given a complete soul, but each half was left with a lasting need for the other. Each was given qualities and abilities unique to itself. Man has spermatozoa; woman has egg. Both are necessary in the continuation of life. The two halves are different from each other, but their basic equality transcends their differences.

Let me tell you a story:

There was once a human who, after a shipwreck, was alone on a desert island. There were no living creatures except plants on the island. The human was very lonely. One day a kitten swam ashore. The human was delighted. The kitten was a cute, cuddly companion. Later, a puppy swam ashore. Again the human was delighted. The puppy followed him around and obeyed his commands. Even later, a cow swam ashore. She gave him milk to drink, and he made butter and cheese. He enjoyed working with the cow, feeding it and cleaning up after it. Then, a horse swam ashore. He was delighted once more. He loved horses and went riding daily. The horse helped him carry things, so that he could build a house and a barn.

One morning he awoke, and another man had been washed ashore after a shipwreck. The man became his friend and companion . . . but he secretly wished that it had been a woman.

This is the end of the story. The point of the story is that the complete companion, as God planned for humanity, would be the beautiful mixture of similarities and opposites which are found in the relationship between male and female.

Oh, I should tell you that there is an addition to the story. One morning two very welcome women swam ashore!

Angelique, in the last letter we talked about the consequences of human disobedience in the Garden of Eden. Some humans have believed that the evil consequences were God's curse. We suggested that evil has its terrible consequences, but that God does not curse humans or any other creature—He has no malice. Thus, it is not true that our Father cursed Eve by making her desire for her husband to increase, or by making her husband rule over her. Women have pain in childbirth for many reasons, including the fact of the evolutionary development of a large brain, thus the large infant head. (A part of God's plan in human development has been this increased size of the brain.)

Wives do desire their husbands, as husbands desire their wives. The desire is good. It is no curse. And on the earth-planet, husbands have indeed ruled over their wives and, in some cases, wives have ruled over their husbands—facts that we angels are desperately trying to help change.

In any event, the Biblical Eden story intended to show that God created male and female as equals, when it suggested that the husband's dominance was a part of Eve's punishment. Male dominance would not have been a punishment for Eve if God had meant to create her inferior to Adam. The dominance would have already been there. Her punishment represented that the intended equality had been taken away from her.

Earth-Christians understand that God's gift of Himself on the cross atoned for—paid for—the sins of Eden. They should therefore realize that in Christ, the original equality of the sexes was restored. As we have said, God did not curse the man and the woman in Eden. But their disobedience had terrible consequences. One of the consequences was that some men want to dominate and abuse women. And some women want to dominate and abuse men. Such dominance and abuse are violations of God's ways.

Angelique, continue to support your young minister in his recognition of God's call of both men and women to His service. Remember, souls are created equal.

Love,
Uncle Gabe

XXVIII

CONTROVERSY

Dear Angelique,

It is amazing how your young minister finds his way into the center of earthly controversy! You say that recently you discovered him in a "protest" march? And he was carrying a sign opposing the creation of more destructive instruments of war? I am in agreement with your young minister. Since humans have discovered how to release the energy of the stars, we of the Hosts have been quite worried about the future of the earth-planet. They have the power to destroy themselves! Sometimes, in my moments of doubt (only God is perfect!), I feel it a pity that God, in His plan for the ultimate Heavenly fellowship, decided to give humans so much freedom and so much intelligence. They really can destroy themselves!

Is it true that your young minister petitioned the leader of his state, asking permission to die in that "electric seat?" It seems that he opposes killing. To make his opposition known, he was offering to die in place of one of his human brothers who had taken the earth-life of a fellow human? I believe they call the crime "murder," and his state punishes the crime of murder by killing the convicted criminal. It has always astounded me that humans seem to believe that by murdering the murderer, they will stop murders! Human minds are capable of better thinking. And human souls are made for loving, not killing.

Angelique, you are doing your guardian work very well. I admire courage in humans, and you are giving good advice and support about courage. The marching and protesting are risky, and not always good methods. But humans must learn to risk what they have, for rightness. The risking is an important part of faith growing.

Our Father calls on certain humans to lead other humans, through risk, to the truths of His eternal love. He has called these humans to be "prophets." Your young minister, with your guidance, is perceiving the truths and is progressing admirably in a prophetic ministry.

Your young minister lives with earth-problems as do all humans. He sees crimes and cries out, with its victims, for it to stop. He sees war and cries out, with its victims, for it to stop. Through his dedication to the Christ and His teachings, he realizes that severe punishment is not the solution for crime. And more terrible weapons are not the solution for war. Severe punishment and terrible weapons are not stopping crime and war. Human hearts are the problem, and they are what must be changed.

Angelique, punishment may seem necessary, now . . . nuclear weapons may seem necessary, now . . . but, I must tell you, God's hope is for different solutions! His plan is for humankind to recognize that the only final cure for sin, crime, and war on earth will come when humans learn to care enough about each other to deal with their sin, crime, and war through the power of good instead of the power of evil. Punishment and weapons of war are instruments of evil.

An "eye for an eye" may be just. It may be fair: equal punishment for the crime. That is human justice. But humans also have the gift of the Divine. Our Father has put His Spirit in them. They have contact with . . . indeed their souls are fashioned by . . . the Divine. They can see. They can understand: Evil is stopped only by good. Evil methods, no matter what the purpose nor how well intentioned the motive, cannot produce final results of good. Whether it is a parent attempting to control a child's behavior, or a government incarcerating a criminal, punishment is used because humans have not found a better way.

Punishment seems necessary to humans who have not discovered redemptive, healing compassion. But when humans discover this compassion and learn how to apply it in their lives, sin and crime and wars do stop! Human solutions will never be complete until humans learn to trust completely in our Father's love.

In the meantime, Angelique, practice angelic patience. Human souls are mortal with the potential of being raised to eternal life. Our heavenly abode is eternal, and our Father has eternity through which to work His miracles.

In His Love,
Uncle Gabe

XXIX

HUMANITY'S WORST CRIME
AND GOD'S HEALING POWER

Dear Angelique,

Oh! What can I say? You have related a story that so touches my heart, that even our angelic experience of God's mercy is tried and tested by the human agony which you have described. Your young minister is counseling in an area of human suffering where all of the hosts of Heaven join in prayers and blessings.

RAPE! Is there a more horrible thought in God's creation? The beautiful young earth-girl was violated in the worst possible way in a moment of madness, passion, violence, and greed . . . by one of God's children-turned-mad. She was only fifteen years of age—a child!

Trusting our heavenly protection in ways we cannot provide, and assuming (as most humans do) that nothing bad could ever happen to her, she ventured out one night, and he grabbed her, threw her to the ground, and took a part of her—a God-given part of her—which can never be given back.

The human female is born virgin. In the human realm, it is a state of purity and innocence which she gladly gives to the human male of her choosing. Our Father gives her the gift as a symbol of divine holiness. It is a part of the gift which He gives to all humans, both male and female, to show them the beauty of the heavenly fellowship. The complete love which humans can experience in the fullness of the male-female relationship is the experience of God. For humans to violate this relationship is to violate

God. Therefore, rape is pure blasphemy, because it is the worst possible abuse of that which is holy.

In order for me to help you advise your young minister in his counseling, let me advise you about the earth-girl and her feelings.

Her feeling of shock is beyond description. At first, the horror is too much, and she will experience a state of stupor with no feelings at all. She will refuse to believe that it has happened. It can not have happened to her! "No! No! It did not happen!"

Then follows pain—hurt—bleeding—a sense of violation—victimized. Did he want to kill her? Is she dead? She might hope so! And she feels emotionally, mentally crushed. It did happen! Worse than death, she has been raped! She knows:

"It did happen to me. Why? Why? Why? I feel dirty. I can not get clean. I will never be clean again. I must scrub myself clean, scrub with a brush, with soap and water, until my skin is raw. But I still feel dirty. Must I forever feel dirty?"

There is anger—deep, abiding anger:

"What right did he have to take that of me which was not his? What right? How can I hurt him? I must get even with him. But where is he? Is he all men? I hate him! There is no good in him. He should be killed . . . tortured and killed! Oh, I can never be myself, again. He stole me from me! He took my life—my soul—my self, and damaged it beyond repair. I hate men for what they have done to me!"

Then, there is guilt:

"There must be something wrong with me—something inherently dirty about me; or else he would not have chosen me. It must have been my fault!"

There are nightmares—those human horror fantasies during sleep, when she relives the terrible experience over and over. The nightmares occur night after night, and the rape experience becomes what she thinks is a permanent part of her life. Thus, all humans of the male sex are to be *suspect*. Their natural passions must be to dominate and to violate. They do not love. They cannot give. They only desire . . . and take what is not theirs. She will say,

"Sex is dirty. All sex is wrong. Love is impossible. I do not need sex. And I will not forgive. I must remember the pain—the horror—so that no man can ever hurt me again. I will make it on my own, alone!"

Angelique, such are the experiences of an earth-girl raped. There is no crime more violent or more demonic. There are other forms of rape, such as the experience of earth-boys who see the horrors of war. Something of God's holiness is violated in them, too. Our task is to know the damage and the dangers—and to stop the workings of evil through the healing powers of God's love.

Angelique, we must help the earth-girl know that some of her reactions to this violation, though natural and understandable, can be very destructive. She will be hard to convince, but she needs to be shown that God's healing can take place in her life and make her whole again. Her life need not be destroyed by this insane act.

Among the earth-girl's destructive reactions are her feelings of guilt. To deal with guilt, we must give her the reassurance that she did not cause this atrocity. She was the victim, not the cause. Guilt should be reserved for the guilty, yet it is one of our enemy's favorite weapons against the innocent. We must help her rediscover the self-esteem which she needs to protect herself from Satan's assault of guilt.

The evil is in the heart and mind of the madman who attacked her. Her beauty, her innocence, and her femininity are God's blessings upon her. Only a madman would desire to violate those blessings.

In addition to her need for protection from the destructiveness of guilt, she needs to know that God's mercy has the power to cleanse and heal. Many humans understand God's mercy to forgive sin. Christ's death on the cross was *God*, taking on the sins of the world. For Christian humans, the cross symbolizes that God can forgive all sins. The forgiveness is unconditional. It does not depend upon human goodness. Humans understand God's mercy to forgive sin.

But God's mercy has another side. The earth-girl feels dirty and wounded. Even as God forgives sin and the sinner, so God's mercy can cleanse and heal the victim of sin.

Sin is evil. It cannot be made good. But God's power is greater than evil. Evil can damage. It can destroy. But God's mercy is stronger. God's mercy can cleanse and heal! It can stop the damage and the destruction, and it can turn them around. One of the magnificent qualities of God's creating is that evil and suffering can be turned around. With His help, evil and suffering can become opportunities through which His Grace works.

When the earth-girl was raped, she was the victim of humanity's worst crime. She felt dirty, used, abused, and assaulted—all of the worst that the evil of the enemy can produce. But her true virginity has not been taken from her, because she is a soul created in the divine image. Her purity, though in a state of danger, is the purity of God, God-given. It is threatened by the rapist's insane act, but there is God's power to heal. God's mercy can cleanse and heal even her feelings of dirtiness and pain. Contrary to the way she feels, she is in God's eyes still holy, still a creation in His image. It is the human mind that sees her as made dirty by the rape.

Many humans understand God's mercy in forgiving sin. They need to understand *the power of God's mercy to cleanse and heal the victims of sin.* The earth-girl raped is a victim of another human's sin. Her feelings of dirtiness and hurt are real. She has been severely wounded. God's love can cleanse and heal her!

The earth-girl, raped, is the victim of the violence of an individual madman. But there is another factor! The society in which she lives is also responsible. Humans as individuals must be held responsible for their acts, but humans are also molded and sometimes driven mad by the terrible pressures from their fellow human beings. In this sense, all humans share in the guilt of the rapist, and the rape victim is paying for the sins of her fellow human beings.

Many earth-years ago, Jesus on the cross paid for the sins of the whole world. His pain and suffering were beyond imagining. He felt alone and in His agony quoted the Psalmist, "My God, my God, why hast thou forsaken me?" (Psalms 22:1). His human nature was crying out for assurance, so great was His suffering. Yet that event was the most holy event in earth's history. It was the divine act of cleansing. His suffering showed the extent of God's intent to save the human race.

The suffering which the earth-girl has experienced can be, through the power of God (on a much smaller scale) a cleanser, too. Humans have the spark of the Divine. In many small ways, by carrying their crosses, they can share in the divine cleansing of the world's sin. Though humans rarely realize it at the time of the suffering, their suffering carries them very close to the heart of God.

We must help humans realize this truth. The realization is crucial because suffering also has the potential for destruction. If left to the enemy, suffering is a terrible demoralizer of souls. Fortunately though, as it takes souls close to the heart of God, suffering places souls in a perfect position for God's activity. We must help these souls reach out and take God's power which is always available to them. It is God's power which changes suffering into holiness.

Finally, we must help the earth-girl know that her innermost desires to love, to touch, and to have companionship with a human male, are good and holy and right. Her assumption that all human males are like the one who violated her, is wrong. The one who violated her, himself a victim of our enemy's lust, was soul-sick and depraved. God did not create human males to be depraved.

God's plan is that human males and females are given equally the same desires, the same needs, the same passions, and the same abilities to love each other. Their ways of expressing these God-given assets vary. But men and women alike are capable of experiencing the divine fellowship through the male-female love relationship. It is our Father's best earth-gift to them.

We must not let this very special earth-girl develop attitudes which will cause her to miss the best of life, the experiences which God has planned for her happiness. One of God's best introductions to the divine fellowship is for her the experience of loving an earth-man, even as for that earth-man, it is the experience of loving her.

Sincerely,
Uncle Gabe

XXX

FUNDAMENTALISM I

Dear Angelique,

You have been asking about a movement in the Church called "fundamentalism." I have heard of it—I have heard of it too much. It gives us great grief in Heaven. Did they not teach you about it at Angel College? I thought that Professor Free Spirit offered a course on Fundamentalism in the Faith Department. Don't tell me they've dropped it from the curriculum! Fundamentalism may be the greatest heresy in the history of the Church! I certainly intend to get in touch with Dr. Verily Verily, the president of our college, to tell him of the great need for instruction to our guardians about fundamentalism.

In the meantime, let me give you some basic information to help you advise your young minister in dealing with the many terrible problems which we and humans face concerning fundamentalism.

Fundamentalism is an extreme conservatism and a legalism. It is a reactionary attitude against change, against newness, and against free thought. It gets its name from an attempt to return to "fundamental" beliefs (among Christians, the original beliefs of the early Church). However, the attempt is a guise to cover up the insecurity which comes from lack of faith. In practice, fundamentalists are rule-makers who think that faith can be a set of rules. Therefore, they create a set of rules, give the rules the sound of faith, and then *substitute their rules for true faith*. Fundamentalists are not really "fundamentalists." They are not seeking a return to fundamentals—original beliefs. They are rule-makers seeking to enforce their own rules. Following rules is easier than developing faith. Therefore, fundamentalism is very attractive to humans searching for a strong faith.

Fundamentalism is a basic mindset that attempts to invade all areas of life. It can enter politics and control governments and nations. As such, it usually has a strong inclination toward dictatorships, violence, and war. It may cry,

"We believe in democratic principles. We want a government for the people."

But it robs the people of their freedom and their sense of worth.

Fundamentalism fears the search for knowledge and scientific inquiry. When the science of astronomy began to look out through telescopes into the universe, fundamentalists tried to stop the astronomers, complaining that their discoveries contradicted traditional religious beliefs. When geology began to study the earth's rocks and the record of earth-life in the rock's fossils, the fundamentalists accused the geologists of being atheists . . . deniers of God, because their discoveries did not always agree with tradition.

The fundamentalist mindset attempts to enter all types of religions and religious organizations. During the time of Jesus on the earth-planet, it became a heretical philosophy among the leaders of the Jews . . . the Scribes, Pharisees, and High Priests in Jerusalem. Their fundamentalism resulted in the crucifixion of Jesus.

In the late 20th Century on the earth-planet, there was a "hostile take-over" of a large Protestant Christian denomination that had its origins in independent thought, nonconformity, and a marvelous belief in "the sufficiency of the human soul in the presence of God." The sad result was a denomination where a few religious leaders determined what persons were required to believe in order to be members of that denomination!

During the early 21st Century, an extreme fundamentalism caused a terrible heresy among Muslims, resulting in terrorism, suicide bombings, and wars.

Fundamentalism is obviously a very dangerous philosophy. Let me describe the original five requirements of the Christian Fundamentalists as they appeared in the late 19th Century. These five requirements were adopted by a group of concerned Christians who came together in New York City in the 1890's.

Requirements of Christian Fundamentalism

1. Inerrant/Infallible Bible, Literally Read

Inerrancy and infallibility of scripture are the central concepts of religious fundamentalism. The word "fundamentalism" suggests "important" and "basic." There is nothing wrong with the word. But in practice, fundamentalism is an intense legalism. And it is a legalism based upon the idea that the Bible was dictated, word for word, by God and must be taken literally.

The particular writings which the earthly church calls "Scripture" or "Bible" are an amazingly good collection of writings documenting events in which our Father has revealed Himself to humans. But this Bible is not the only document which holds the revelations of God. Many humans have received God in their lives, and many have written about these experiences. Our Father is constantly making himself known to humans, directly and indirectly, through the beauties of His creative Spirit and through the spiritual workings of guardians like yourself. God has endless means.

When humans receive God openly, amazing things happen. They speak of miracles, and they record the events. Their Bible is such a record—of marvelous value to them and to us. To infer that these human documents, divinely inspired as they are, might be without error or be completely sure, is to suggest that the human documents are God. But they are not God, and to mistake human records—even the records of divine events—for God, is idolatry. It is extremely dangerous. "Thou shall not make for thyself a graven image."

2. Virgin Birth

For centuries, Christian humans have believed the Christmas story told by the two Gospel writers, Matthew and Luke. In these accounts, God sent His Son to enter the world of humanity as a child, Jesus, born to a virgin mother with the Holy Spirit as the child's father. Fundamentalists insist that true Christians are required to believe this story. It matters not that the two other Gospel writers, Mark and John, said nothing of a virgin birth. They assume that God entered the world at Jesus' baptism. Paul, the great human missionary, never mentioned the Christmas story as a part of his instructions to new Christians. We assume that he knew nothing about a virgin birth.

Therefore, this fundamentalist belief would suggest that Mark, John, and Paul do not meet the requirements of being Christian.

Nonsense! That the Son was sent—the Incarnation—is the divine act to be believed. How our Father fully incorporated the divine in human flesh, humans will never completely understand. For fundamentalists to demand allegiance to one particular understanding is the very kind of Pharisaism which crucified the Son, Jesus.

To believe in the virgin birth is a Christian tradition. There is certainly no wrong in believing it. But fundamentalists make the believing of it a necessity, a requirement. To make it a requirement for being a Christian is wrong! (We will speak more about Pharisaism later.)

3. Substitutionary Atonement
    Substitutionary Atonement is a historic Christian belief. It expresses the love of God, taking the sins of humanity as His own, and paying for those sins, Himself. God became a human, Jesus of Nazareth, and walked the earth. Because the demands of divine love challenged human religious traditions, the leaders of those traditions ordered Jesus to be arrested, tried, and executed as a criminal—though innocent. His death was God's sacrificing of Himself for humanity. Thus, Jesus was a substitute sacrifice, atoning (paying) for the sins of the world, because God was uniquely in him.

Christian humans explain God as a *Trinity*. They speak of God's human form as the "Son." It is very difficult for humans to understand how God can be Father: Creator, the ruler of the universe; and be Son: a human, Jesus, walking the earth planet to redeem it; and also be Holy Spirit: in their hearts sustaining their lives with the joy of His love. God is, of course, all of these, Father, Son, and Holy Spirit . . . a Trinity. Yet, God is one. His nature is a unity. Father, Son, and Holy Spirit are one.

Fundamentalists' erroneous interpretation of substitutionary atonement is that of an angry father sending his gentle son to pay for someone else's crimes. The son cares for the criminals—the sinners. The father does not. He only wants payment. He is an angry vengeful, demanding judge. The son offers himself as a substitute sacrifice to appease the angry father.

This fundamentalist suggestion that the Son died to appease an angry God is a grave human error! It is a misunderstanding of the Trinity. It divides God into three Gods. It would suggest that God caused Jesus' death.

Humans crucified the Son. God did not! Of course, the risk was known by God. But the important truth is that it was God in Jesus on that cross. The sacrifice was the ultimate proof of God's love—His complete love. The fundamentalist interpretation twists this complete gift of God into the suggestion that God is a bad parent and an irresponsible tyrant. It is enough to make our Father angry! (Yes, He does express anger, but never for destruction; only as an expression of His mercy.)

4. Belief in (Supernatural) Miracles
One of the requirements of the fundamentalists is the belief in miracles. They believe miracles to be God's intervention into the human world. The subject of miracles is a very complex issue. I will devote a whole letter to it, later. At this point, let me simply say that here, as in other areas, fundamentalism leaves little room for thought or discussion or disagreement. One must accept and believe without question. Our Father wants humans to think, discuss, and disagree . . . in love.

5. Physical Resurrection of Jesus
Fundamentalists require a literal belief in the physical resurrection of Jesus. His physical body—the one he had on earth—is believed by fundamentalists to have died, to have come back to life again, and to have been resurrected into Heaven, there to exist eternally.

As with the virgin birth, it is the requirement of a particular belief that is in question. Though many Christians have understood the resurrection of Christ as including the resurrection of the physical body, most understand the spiritual resurrection to be the more important concept. The Apostle Paul was given special visions of Heaven and wrote about these visions. He described resurrection as being with a spiritual, not physical body . . . the mortal or physical taking on the immortal or spiritual and eternal.

Our Father's way with the union of physical and spiritual is a mystery to humans! Indeed, it is a mystery that we in heavenly circles do not completely understand. In humans, spiritual healing often occurs even as physical bodies are dying—and spiritual death takes place in souls with apparently healthy bodies. Humans tend to separate the physical and the spiritual, when there is no such separation. (Some even think that the act of sexual love need have no connection with spiritual love. Impossible! The two are mysteriously but inevitably linked.)

The resurrection of Jesus is one of the mysteries in which we get a glimpse of the link between the physical and the spiritual. The Son's physical body died. The marvelous transformation of physical and spiritual—the resurrection—is a mystery. Truth uses physical vessels, yet is more than the physical. Love unites male humans with female humans and in a physical act, creates new physical bodies . . . babies. Yet love transcends the physical act, and the babies possess individual souls . . . much more than just physical bodies. Humans want to believe in a physical resurrection because they want to believe that they will recognize their loved ones in Heaven, and they cannot understand how spiritual beings can know each other. (They think *seeing* is *believing*!) Faith is often strengthened by physical events, yet if that faith is dependent upon those events for the proof of its reality, it ceases to be faith.

Faith, truth, and love are always beyond (more than) the physical, even as on the human level they always interact with the physical. In Heaven, the spiritual rules completely. The spiritual is the ultimate reality. But for humans on the earth-planet, this reality—this resurrection—will always be a mystery. Fundamentalism's demand for a literal belief in the physical resurrection can cause humans to miss the beauty of the mystery and the reality of the spiritual.

Angelique, these are the five "rules" of fundamentalism. The rules are not necessarily wrong. I hope that I have made it clear that the wrong often lies in the interpretation. I also hope that my comments will help you in your guardianship.

We really must do something about the condition of our Angel College! It seems to be becoming just an on-line business school!

Love,
Uncle Gabe

XXXI

FUNDAMENTALISM II

Dear Angelique,

My last letter about fundamentalism must have made quite an impact on you. Your return letter is filled with commments and questions and concerns about the way this movement is affecting your young minister and the people with whom he is working. Yes, there are other characteristics which fundamentalism has adopted in recent years. These characteristics are the natural result of the directions of belief taken by the original five requirements. And they are just as dangerous! They deserve our study and concern. There are four of these characteristics. Let me describe them for you.

1. Exclusivism: God Loves Only a "Few"

Fundamentalists tend to believe that very few humans will ever make it to Heaven . . . that God's love is for only a few. They believe that only Christians have Grace and, therefore, Heaven (and, actually, only *their kind* of Christians).

Several earth-years ago, a very pompous Christian human declared to the world that God could not hear the prayers of Jews. Humans of good will, everywhere, cried out in shock (even as Father Abraham and God chuckled in bemused disgust here in Heaven!) For a Christian human to think that God saves only Christians, or, more to the point, saves only His kind of Christians, is the epitome of religious conceit. As we said in our letter about the United Way, God loves all humans, and His purpose is the salvation of all. That pompous Christian human, in defense of his comment, quoted Jesus as saying,

"I am the way, and the truth, and the life; no one comes to the Father, but by me." (John 14:6)

"Mr. Pompous" apparently perceived that Jesus meant to say that God had established Jesus as a kind of gatekeeper for Heaven. The idea is that Jesus must approve prayers, or that prayers must be "in Jesus' name," in order for the prayers to be passed on to God.

Sheer nonsense!

Must we use the name "Jesus" in all our prayers? Is the name "Jesus" a secret password to enter Heaven or to catch our Father's ear? Does God care only for Christians? Is salvation only for them?

Certainly not!

God's love is for all humans and His salvation is planned for all. His compassion is complete and leaves no soul outside its bounds.

Christ is God . . . the Word . . . the Spirit-Idea. He was in the beginning. All things were created through Him. The Word became flesh—human flesh—and was born, grew up, lived, taught, and died as the man, Jesus. God lived in the form of an earth-person to show humans His light, His love, and that His plan is for all. No one comes to the Father but by Jesus, because Jesus and the Father are one. It is an invitation to all, not an exclusion of "sinners" or "non-Christians" or any other soul. God hears all prayers! He hears prayers in Jesus' name. He hears prayers from humans who never heard of Jesus. Jesus, the Christ, was the "Son" form of the "Father." But Son and Father are one. Jesus was saying that no humans come to God but by God. It was not an exclusivist statement, but rather a statement of God's inclusive plan of salvation for all humans through the death and resurrection of Christ, God's gift of Himself to the world.

There are honest, good humans who have been led to believe that our Father loves only a few—His "chosen" ones. But God became flesh and visited the earth to tell humans that this idea is not true. God's compassion includes all. He pours His love out on all: the good and the bad, the rich and the poor, the young and the old . . . and all others. His special favorites are often those who suffer. He promises that their suffering will lead them to strength and joy. But His total aim is to give His kingdom to His children—His whole creation.

2. Heaven or Hell: God's Only Choices When Humans Die
    Fundamentalists believe that at death, human souls are sent to one of only two places. It is for eternity, and it is either Heaven or Hell. It is as if they believe that God's choices are limited by their small, narrow theological doctrines!

    There are other Christians who have suggested that at the time of death, most humans are neither good enough for Heaven nor bad enough for Hell. So, where can they go? These Christians have developed a belief in a state of the soul which they call Purgatory. To purge means to cleanse. In Purgatory, souls can gain merit and forgiveness, so that they may at a future time enter Heaven. The concept is a reasonable one, based on essential Christian teachings of God's mercy.

    Fundamentalists want to simplify things (though life and eternity are never simple). Thus, they have a need to understand eternity in terms of "either-or." They want to believe that eternity will be good to them, and so they conceive of Heaven . . . Paradise. (Since our Father does have marvelous plans for their souls, their ideas of Heaven are partially true.) They also like to think that their enemies will be punished, and so they embrace the idea of Hell.

    Humans have been given real freedom. They can choose or reject all forms of goodness and all forms of evil. When they accept the gifts of God's love, the acceptance, called faith, leads them to Heaven. But they can choose selfishness instead of love. They can choose many forms of destructiveness and evil. These choices lead to Hell.

    God's eternity is not limited to only two choices. God's eternity has eternal possibilities. Heaven and Hell are His extremes. Human death is a threshold through which human souls pass on the way to the myriad possibilities for life and growth and learning to love—or death and shrinkage and learning to hate. But God will never give up on any soul, even a soul in Hell! He will woo it until He has won it to the way of complete love. It may take an eternity!

3. Legalism: the Rule-Makers
    Fundamentalists say,
    "All you have to do is join the right church and believe the right things."

In contrast, Saint Paul, when referring to the demand of certain early Christians who wanted acceptance of the Jewish law as a requirement for Christianity, said,

"For freedom Christ has set us free; stand fast therefore, and do not submit again to a yoke of slavery." (Galatians 5:1)

Legalism is the reduction of religious faith to a set of rules. Our son, Moses, brought the Jews out of slavery in Egypt, and built them into a nation, through the inspiration of God's laws. Those Ten Commandments or laws formed a foundation for earth-people's lives. The laws established basic rules for their relationships with God and with each other. With this foundation, our Father has been leading people toward faith and a right heart ever since. When faith takes over a human life, and human hearts hold attitudes of love, the foundation rules cease to be necessary. Saint Paul discovered the joy of faith in his experience of Christ, and always thereafter realized that a return to living by rules alone would be a return to the yoke of slavery. Faith sets souls free.

But always there have been humans who confuse laws for God, and thus worship the laws instead of worshiping God. These are the rule-makers. God wants love-givers. In Jesus' days on the earth-planet, a particular group of rule-makers were called Pharisees. Because Jesus questioned their rules in favor of faith, right attitudes, and compassion, these Pharisees became the leaders in the plot to crucify Jesus. Fundamentalists are rule-makers, like the Pharisees. They understand very little of faith and the matters of the heart.

4. Anti-Reason, Anti-Science

Fundamentalists say,

"Don't listen to those college professors! They'll take you straight to Hell!"

Fundamentalism, in its extremely conservative stance, is very suspicious of any group of humans that questions the complete acceptance of its beliefs. It demands that all humans follow without question. Reason and science, disciplines that question religious traditions and dogmatism, are perceived as against faith and therefore against God.

Angelique, God's universe was created upon divine laws of reason. When God made humans, He instilled in them the ability to think. He instilled in them the ability to perceive and use divine reason. Science is a method by which humans use their gift of reason in their search for truth. Thus, with science through reason, human's search for truth closely parallels God's revelations of truth to them. God's gifts to humans include these two ways of finding truth: discovery through the use of reason and discovery through the receiving of God's revelations. Both are gifts from God. When humans empirically (sight, sound, touch, smell, and taste) explore the world around them, they do so by reason. When humans receive God's revelations, they do so by faith. When they use reason and faith together, their lives become whole with the fullness of these divine gifts. However, the use of reason requires that humans question and doubt traditional beliefs. This process is necessary for human growth.

Fundamentalists attack anything that questions their established rules and beliefs. On the earth-planet in early New England America, Puritan Christians gave the name of "witch" to anyone who was different from themselves or questioned their ways. Then they burned them! Fundamentalists in this day on earth burn books! I think that they would rather burn people!—especially college professors!

Angelique, I suppose that we should consider that these two letters represent a "crash" course in fundamentalism. I hope this information is useful to you in helping your young minister deal with this serious heresy. You will be happy to hear that I have had correspondence from Dr. Verily Verily of our Angel College, and he promises to restore "Fundamentalism 423" to the curriculum, preparing guardians for dealing with fundamentalism on the earth-planet.

Love,
Uncle Gabe

XXXII

MIRACLES

Dear Angelique,

As I said to you in my first letter about fundamentalism, the subject of miracles deserves a separate letter. Humans do have many differing ideas about the way God works in their lives. One of the rules of fundamentalism is that humans must believe the Biblical accounts of miracles. They interpret miracles as mysterious, even magical interventions of God into the workings of the world. Then they demand belief in these miracles as a requirement to be a Christian.

God seems, by this interpretation, to be a God who can act on any whim, because He is God. Such a concept of God's activities allows the possibility of God's violating His own laws. But God never violates His own laws! God is consistent. God is not a God of whims. God does not "play favorites." And God does not choose to answer some human prayers while ignoring others.

Let me offer an example: Joe and Sam have terminal cancer. Joe is a Christian and Sam is an Atheist, so God miraculously heals Joe. No! No! No! No! God loves them both equally. (Actually, as I have discussed in my letter to you about jealousy, there is a sense in which God loves Sam more.) The beauty of the Christian Faith is that it has at its heart an understanding of God's love. Thus Joe does have an advantage, if he has caught the message. He may be more open to the healing powers which God makes available to *all* humans, because he knows about the healing powers.

God hears all human prayers and answers all human prayers, according to what He knows is best for each human. God exercises His will, acts in the affairs of humans, and surrounds all humans with His love. To those who discover that love and respond to that love, the truth of God's miracles is revealed. Divine love and divine power in the forms of healing, purpose in life, fellowship, and eternal life are among the miracles.

The questions here are very important: What constitutes a miracle? And how does God perform a miracle? Our definition of miracle is,

"God is doing something which no one else can do."

Creation is a miracle. Life is a miracle. The gift and use of intelligence are miracles (as when Moses used his understanding of God's will and God's weather, winds, and tide to cross the Red Sea). The love of God is the greatest miracle.

Yes, God does perform miracles. Theses miracles are not violations of God's laws. But His ability to use His compassion, His powers, and His laws, is always beyond human understanding. God has many ways of exercising His will for good, and often these ways appear to humans to be supernatural miracles. God is supernatural! But if humans could understand God more fully, they would realize that God is making use of His laws, not violating them.

Biblical accounts suggest that Jesus had miraculous healing powers. God in Christ healed in ways humans do not understand. Angels do not fully understand, either. Healing is one of God's miracles, and Jesus had full knowledge of healing. He used His divine powers always for human good. Jesus was the great physician!

Angelique, isn't it amusing that when Jesus cured a disease, gave sight to the blind or the ability to walk to the lame, humans called it divine intervention, a miracle. Yet when a new life is created—when a human baby is born—they consider it quite natural and claim to have done it all by themselves! Sometimes they are glad, and sometimes they are not.

When they awaken each day, a special gift of life from our Father, they take the gift quite for granted, and often arise from their sleep in a grouchy frame of mind! And when friendships develop between humans, they assume that it is their own doings.

Angels preserve us!

All good is from God, directly or indirectly from God, inspired by God. Goodness is always a miracle. The Biblical miracles are normal divine events.

Love,
Uncle Gabe

XXXIII

TV EVANGELISM I

Dear Angelique,

"Television!" And "Media!" These words that appear in your last letter signal trouble which your young minister must face. They represent very recent additions to the human scene!

Through the methods which humans call "science," wonderful new forms of communications have been developed. These new forms can be used in serving our Father, but as your letter outlined, some very serious problems exist. Through television and other forms of mass media, spokespersons for religion are representing Christianity in very confusing ways. The members of your young minister's congregation, and, as a matter of fact, humans all over the earth-planet, are becoming confused about the central truths of God's ways. I believe I can help you with these problems. They are related to problems that have been with us for centuries.

We must be alert to the means by which humans abuse religion. Religion, human's worship, is a very powerful force which can be used for good or evil. Humans who follow the enemy use religion to become wealthy and to gain personal power. They use it to build their own empires, to satisfy lust, and to satisfy many other forms of greed. The abuses of religion are usually very subtle, and self-seeking prophets and evangelists always have been the masters of subtle abuse. These television evangelists of whom you spoke seem to continue the mastery.

Let me outline the abuses, which are many:

The emotion of guilt is a very painful and destructive human emotion. Because religion is always involved in the search for righteousness, the evangelist can use his own ideas of righteousness in ways which are intended to make his listeners feel guilty. These listeners are told that they are "against God" or that they are "creatures of Satan." The evangelist then creates a plan which he guarantees will bring forgiveness, salvation, and freedom from the pain of guilt. With the need to be relieved of the pain, his listeners eagerly accept the plan which he has invented and imposed upon them. When the evangelist controls the blueprint of the plan, he controls his listeners, and can use them in support of his quest for power.

In much the same way the evangelist can paint a picture of a terrible God—full of wrath for His enemies and exercising His power for their destruction. He can paint a nasty picture of eternal torment in Hell! The same plan which he has devised to clear the guilty can be used to calm the fearful. In both cases, the guilty and the fearful, the evangelist's devised plan is his means of manipulating his listeners.

His listeners are encouraged to develop a religious devotion to him, the self-appointed "cult" leader, or to the organization which he establishes. This devotion to a human "cult" leader becomes a substitute for rightful devotion to God.

You mentioned that one such television evangelist told his listeners that if they did not send him enough money (and he demanded and exorbitant amount), God would end his life and take him from them.

Maybe God should have! His is the worst form of hypocrisy. He is suggesting that his personal health and safety are in jeopardy, unless his listeners' generosity satisfies a relentlessly demanding God. He is using his supposed familiarity with God to cheat and lie to those listeners. Even more serious is the fact that he is portraying God as a terrible tyrant.

False prophets and false evangelists through the centuries have portrayed God as a power-hungry, wrathful tyrant. They have said that He does not love any beings except those who obey His dictatorial whims.

Jesus' message to humans was,

"God is not like that!"

True obedience to our Father is the free and willing desire to love as He loves, to have mercy on all His creatures, and to trust in His plan for His Kingdom. God's Kingdom is where He creates children who grow up to inherit that Kingdom, because their love coincides with His love, and their concern is for others before self.

Another television evangelist, I am told, made the remark, "I love the Jews. Many of them are my good friends. What a pity that they are all going to Hell!"

This evangelist went on to say that belief in Jesus Christ is the only salvation. The Jews have had their chance to accept Jesus as their Messiah. Since they have not accepted Him, God has no alternative but to send them to Hell.

What amazing conceit! This evangelist is telling his listeners that he is better than God! He (the evangelist) loves the Jews. He would not send them to Hell. But the god that he describes would send them to Hell—gladly! By his god's rule (that salvation is only for those who believe in Jesus—a human rule attributed to God), his god can neither love the Jews nor save them. He must send them to Hell! The evangelist is better than God!

Angelique, our Father loves all humans. He made their souls. He loves each soul. He plans the salvation of all souls. He has given them freedom to reject Him, and many do, in many ways, and follow Satan to Hell! But God has eternity to surround them with His love, and finally, to win them back. His love to the world through Jesus Christ is His great work of salvation. But He has been saving Jews and Hindus and Buddhists and Muslims, and Christians, etc., etc., etc., for centuries. God's ways of salvation are unnumbered. There are human souls in every community on the earth-planet who know what goodness is. They follow that goodness regardless of religious affiliation. Imagine God sending good souls to Hell because they do not know about Jesus Christ!

Unthinkable!

Compassion is the center of all true religion, because compassion is the center of God. True allegiance to Christ is to follow the way of compassion.

This evangelist would replace compassion with narrow-mindedness and bigotry. True evangelism is the preaching of the "good news" that God loves us. This evangelist would change it to the "bad news!" After preaching his bad news, he informed his listeners that they were $12 million (American money) short of reaching God's goal for his television ministry. Angelique, God's goals are very different from this evangelist's price tag.

You mentioned in your letter that another one of these evangelists has announced that God cannot hear the prayers of the Jews. Our Father would be very surprised to hear that, having listened to their prayers for over four thousand earth-years! (You will remember that I discussed the matter of God's hearing the prayers of Jews in my second letter to you about fundamentalism.)

All through human history there have been individuals who have perverted the most precious gifts of God. They have used His gifts for evil purposes. For example, God has given all humans a wonderful potential for loving. When this potential is directed toward God or souls in need, it becomes worship. It becomes Heaven. When it is directed toward selfish ends, it becomes Hell.

Some evangelists, as they sell out to the enemy, learn to use other humans' potential for loving as an opening for their control of those loving humans. They become masters at turning this potential for loving into a loyalty to themselves. Then they turn that loyalty, that love which their followers have, into hate. They can lead them to hate people who are different in their religious beliefs; to hate people who are different in their racial or national background; to hate any individual or any group that the evangelist wishes to select as the object of the attack. Through the cunning use of the human ability to love, the love is turned to hate, thus leading humans to follow Satan while they think they are following God. They believe that they are lovingly and loyally following one of God's people, when indeed, they are following one of Satan's.

Angelique, the media—radio and television—are very good means of communicating. Heaven knows that on the earth-planet, good means of communicating are needed! There is nothing wrong with using radio and television to tell the great message of God's love, but beware of the abuses.

Love,
Uncle Gabe

XXXIV

TV EVANGELISM II

Dear Angelique,

I am glad that you found my last letter interesting and useful. Your comment about the difficulty which humans have in distinguishing between the true evangelists and the fraudulent ones suggests to me that additional comments may be helpful.

The problem is the selfish human desire for power and money and possessions. Humans have found so many ways of corrupting those things which are good. As we have suggested, radio and television can be very good means of communicating the truth of God's ways. But there are evangelists who are using radio and television for their own selfish purposes. Let me list some ways to distinguish between the genuine and the fraudulent ones:

First, watch for an over-interest in money. If on these radio and television shows, the evangelist uses an unusual amount of time and energy raising money, beware! The evangelist gains amazing power when he becomes the center of attention before crowds of listening souls. It is an easy temptation for abuse.

Humans tend to worship religious leaders, even though the task of the religious leader is to lead humans to the worship of God. Thus it is very easy for an evangelist to "use" the worshiping crowds to acquire personal wealth. The television evangelist can beg his congregation to give money to support his "great work." He can call his people to a lifestyle of generosity and concern for the needs of others . . . a lifestyle of moderation or even sacrifice . . . while at the same time, he himself is amassing great wealth, expensive possessions, and luxurious houses with gold plated plumbing! God's money which should be used to help human need is easily diverted to selfish greed.

No human should make a donation to any evangelist, unless that evangelist is willing to let it be known how he uses the donation. He should have a budget, and the budget should be published.

Second, watch out for scare tactics. Humans frighten easily and are ready prey for religious leaders who portray our loving Father as a mean, vengeful tyrant. With vivid descriptions of burning torment throughout eternity, in a Hell from which there is no escape, some evangelists try to terrify their listeners into supporting their ministry. Instead of preaching Christ's message of endless love, they preach fear.

With this portrayal, the evangelist can lure humans into joining his organization, giving him money, and following him in his ministry of self-serving, not God-serving. It is an interesting philosophical question, Angelique, if Satan himself pretended to be God, and convinced humans to follow him, would those humans, while thinking that they are worshiping God, end up in Hell? Remember, even if they do, God's mercy is endless and can always redeem lost souls. The point is, however, scare tactics are Satan's methods, not God's. Help your young minister to develop ways of protecting his human friends from these fearsome evangelists. The truth of God's love is the best protection.

Third, there is the danger that the evangelist can reduce the religious experience to a form of entertainment, and thus to make his followers think that worship is merely another kind of recreation. Worship is an essential in human life (angel life, too). Without true worship, souls wither and die. Yet often the evangelist's underlying message is that worship is of no importance except as a setting in which he gains support for his crusade. He goes to great expense and effort to stage a grand production. He "plays" with his audience and puts on a big "show." Worship is reduced to entertainment.

Angelique, God is the only One who saves, and He has already done it! Entertainment may be very good, but it is no substitute for worship. Sometimes the evangelist leads humans to believe that God needs our worship for His survival. Worship is not for God's benefit. It is for ours— God's creatures—yes, even angels! It is for our good. Worship teaches us to love God who already loves us. When we open ourselves to love God, we become what we were made to be: creatures who love each other. To love each other, and stop wars, and stop hate, and stop the terrible exploitation of one another is what God made us to become.

Fourth, beware of the judgmental evangelist. Many evangelists send their imagined enemies to Hell along with an amazing array of other good souls. They establish a religion of righteousness and pronounce their judgment on all who fall from their righteous grace. The great irony is that often we discover that they are violating the very rules with which they condemn others. Jesus proclaims to all humans,

"Judge not that you be not judged."

God is the only true Judge, and His judgment is mercy.

Fifth, beware of the evangelist who has contempt for the processes of education and training. Humans who are genuinely sincere in their desire to serve our Father are consistently humble about their lack of knowledge and understanding. They contemplate God's magnificence and know that their own experience of God is but a fleeting glimpse. Their mortal minds can comprehend so little of His glory. To experience God is, for all of us creatures, a humbling experience. Therefore, it is natural for humans who wish to serve Him to realize their need to seek the knowledge that comes with education. They must seek the best available training for their great task.

Angelique, it was reported to me that one of the evangelists, speaking before a television audience of thousands, said,

"My Catholic friends tell us that Saint Peter went to Rome and preached there and was executed by the Roman emperor and was buried there. They claim that their great cathedral is built over his tomb . . . Well, the Catholics can believe what they want, but as for me, I will believe the Bible. And the Bible, in the Epistle of Peter, says that Peter was in Babylon."

My nephew, this evangelist gains great support for his "ministry" by teaching hatred of religious groups who believe differently from himself. He makes repeated attacks upon the Roman Catholics. But for him to flaunt his ignorance before his audience and use his own ignorance as a tool for the spreading of his hatred, gives me great grief. The truth is that Babylon, that wicked earth-city, was destroyed by Persia in the year 482 B.C. There was no Babylon in the time of Saint Peter. Christians used the name "Babylon" to describe their great enemy, the city of Rome!

My point is that this evangelist, if he had prepared himself with only the basics of education for his task of preaching, would have known about

Babylon. His lack of respect for education and educated people is a sign of his lack of respect for God. His allegiance is to the enemy. Beware of those who mock the processes of education.

Sixth, beware of the evangelist who abuses the divine power of healing. I have many reports of humans who claim to have the power to heal. Angelique, only God can heal! Any human who claims to hold this power is a fraud! God pours His healing powers upon humans constantly. A simple scratch of their body's skin-cover could not mend if it were not for the divine healing which is a part of His gift of life. Some humans study and do research to learn and practice the art of medicine, which is the discovery of God's way with healing. Other humans seek the power of faith, and through faith make contact with God's healing powers. But any human who claims to be a healer through his own power is self-centered, not God-centered and is, as I say, a fraud. Beware!

Angelique, the God-given task for humans is to develop the natural ability to love and to distinguish love from hate . . . good from evil. Some evangelists spend their lives teaching and preaching the great love of God. Others spend their lives learning to exploit their fellow humans and abusing the great gifts of God. Help your human to recognize the difference.

True evangelism is a wonderful thing! After all, it has the word "angel" at its center! The "evangel" is a message. In Christianity, it is the message of "Good News," the "Gospel." It is the good news that God loves His creation—His whole creation. It is the good news that God plans the salvation of all of His creation—all souls. God's love is forever.

The true evangelist is a messenger—a messenger of this news of God's endless love, mercy, and compassion . . . and His intent to redeem all, even the worst of sinners, even the fraudulent evangelist!

Affectionately,
Uncle Gabe

XXXV

VICTORY

Dear Angelique,

The enemy has seen defeat! It may be only one small defeat in one seemingly insignificant place, but the choirs of Heaven are rejoicing! The slow, patient work of our Hosts is having marvelous results, and I speak for the Archangelic Hosts in sending our blessings to you for your part in the good work. You have led your young minister to make a courageous stand against the corrupt, selfish leadership which has controlled his denomination. It was a dangerous thing for him to do. Following dreams is always dangerous. He may lose his position as minister in his church, and he may lose many friends. But he saw a wrong, and he has made a stand against it. It was a feat of great courage. Your part was to support the courage. You must continue to do so.

It is really no surprise in this time of awakening for humans, that God's people, who have carried the banner of freedom and brotherhood and sisterhood and love through the centuries, are now experiencing some of the results of their great work.

Human greed for power, position, and possessions, through the constant seduction of the enemy, has attacked the Church in all ages, and from all sides. Many times that greed has gained dominance even among our Father's people. Elijah and Amos and Isaiah and Jeremiah saw God's people corrupted and wanted to run from the corruption. But instead, they answered our Father's call and cried out against the evils. God's Son was sent into a terrible time, when His favorites were being led by rule-makers instead of love-givers. The rule-makers are like the fear groups. We have spoken of both in earlier letters. Because they believe God to be mean and vengeful, they fear Him and each other. To structure their lives against this fearful world, they make rules—strict rules for life—and proclaim the rules as God's rules. The rule-makers and the fear groups, thinking that they could confine God in their holy scroll (their list of rules), sought to kill the Son, because He broke out of the confines of their rule-making prison, and called others to follow Him out to freedom.

Since then, many times greedy people have gained control of His Church. There is corruption in your young minister's church. The leadership of his denomination has made the "institution" which they call "Church"—and the control of that institution—more important than the people! God's concern is not for institutions! It is the individual soul that is everything! The true Church is the gathering of souls—souls dedicated to our Father's love. In your young minister's Church, greedy people have gained control. In the earth-planet's history it has happened many times. Yet seemingly insignificant monks and priests, empowered from on high, and field workers and coal miners, catching visions of God's Truth, have stood against the corruption. Often they have fought bravely and lost. Often the heavens have opened with the glory of their victories.

Today a victory has come on the floor of the Church Convention. Angelique, by your patient and constant lifting up of visions of equality and human worth before your young minister, you have led him to follow his great dream for his Church. One brave young minister has stood against selfish leadership and its followers, and God's Hosts are shouting for joy. In the broader view of things, it is only a small victory, but victories are happening in many places. The final victory will be a long time in coming; but our Parent God created time, you know!

And God works! In the midst of all, courageous leaders, ministers, and church members have quietly kept themselves open to the workings of our Father. The Church, God's people, has remained alive. Humans, however influenced by corruption, all have been endowed with the spark of God. They can see truth. They can understand truth. They can know compassion. And they will respond to goodness. Remember that our Father created them good, like Himself.

For many centuries, even the most loyal followers of God did not believe that the demonic institution of slavery could ever be stopped. Surely human nature would always have master and slave! But some hoped. And some believed. And all followers of God knew that slavery had always been wrong! Through the patient workings of God's Spirit, human dreams caused slavery to cease! And now, the enemy's favorite trumps of racism and caste and discrimination are suffering defeat at every turn. Young and old are seeing their God in each other. Rich and poor are breaking down barriers to greet each other in love. Men and women are looking at each other compassionately as equals. And nation is seeking conversation with nation.

Wars ... one ... day ... will ... cease!

But, today, the clergy and laity of your young minister's church are knowing their equality and determining their own decisions and goals; and the church, there, is alive again!

Rejoice with trumpet sound,
Uncle Gabe, with love.

RICHARD VERNON SHRIVER —BIOGRAPHY—

R ichard Vernon Shriver was born in Nashville, Tennessee, the second of three sons of Thomas A. and Attie Gene Shriver. His father was a highly honored presiding judge of the Tennessee Court of Appeals. His education was in the public schools through the twelfth grade, and his bachelor's degree is in Philosophy from Vanderbilt University. His Master of Divinity degree also is from Vanderbilt. He is an ordained minister in the United Methodist Church, having served churches in Tennessee, Wisconsin, and England for thirty-two years.

Dr. Shriver continued his education in history, music, and Christian Education in the graduate schools of Vanderbilt, Peabody College, Scarritt College, Wisconsin State University, and Middle Tennessee State University, and earned his doctorate in Education and Theology at the Divinity School of Vanderbilt University.

He has been active in radio and television as a regular guest on Nashville's Channel 5 TV, Lebanon, Tennessee's Channel 66 TV, and Nashville's WLAC Radio. He is the "permanent" guest on the award winning nationally aired television and radio show, "We Believe," a Roman Catholic sponsored show.

The Gabriel Letters, was first published in 1990. This new edition has been completely revised. Dr. Shriver's second book, *Gold To Refine*, was published in 2005, and his third, *The Return of Gabriel*, in 2006. He presently is Professor of Philosophy and Religion at Cumberland University in Lebanon, Tennessee and is Adjunct Professor of Religious Studies at Volunteer State College in Gallatin, Tennessee. He lives in Gallatin with his wife, Joy. They have two grown children: son, Colin, and daughter, Kendal who is married to Todd Cathey.

A SHORT SUMMARY

I stumbled on the idea of writing letters from an archangel advising a young guardian, in an introduction to C. S. Lewis' *Screwtape Letters*. I wanted to find a way of looking at our human problems from a divine perspective. It has been a marvelous experience of standing back and imagining that I can see the world through angel eyes. It is an impossible task, of course, but the amazing result for me has been a sense of objectivity and good will.

The intended purpose of the letters is to take seriously the idea of God's complete love. This idea is the center of Christianity. It is Jesus' message, and it is St. Paul's "good news."

We live in an age when institutions of religion are taking a beating—from the media, from popular fiction in books and cinema, from those who proclaim cheap or distorted theology, and from our obsessive desire for wealth, power, and material things. The idea of an ideal church is still our hope: a community of people gathered out of a love of God and a concern for each other, to serve their community and their world. These letters offer advice in creating such an ideal church.

-Richard V. Shriver